CARTESIAN METHOD AND THE PROBLEM OF REDUCTION

Cartesian Method and the Problem of Reduction

EMILY R. GROSHOLZ

CLARENDON PRESS · OXFORD
1991

Oxford University Press, Walton Street, Oxford OX2 6DP
Oxford New York Toronto
Delhi Bombay Calcutta Madras Karachi
Petaling Jaya Singapore Hong Kong Tokyo
Nairobi Dar es Salaam Cape Town
Melbourne Auckland
and associated companies in
Berlin Ibadan

Oxford is a trade mark of Oxford University Press

Published in the United States
by Oxford University Press, New York

© Emily R. Grosholz, 1991

All rights reserved. No part of this publication may be reproduced,
stored in a retrieval system, or transmitted, in any form or by any means,
electronic, mechanical, photocopying, recording, or otherwise, without
the prior permission of Oxford University Press

British Library Cataloguing in Publication Data
Grosholz, Emily R.
Cartesian method and the problem of reduction.
1. French philosophy. Descartes, René, 1596–1650
I. Title
194
ISBN 0–19–824250–6

Library of Congress Cataloging in Publication Data
Grosholz, Emily, 1950–
Cartesian method and the problem of reduction / Emily R. Grosholz
p. cm.
Includes bibliographical references and index.
1. Descartes, René, 1596–1650—Contributions in methodology.
2. Methodology—History—17th century. 3. Analysis (Philosophy)—
History—17th century. I. Title.
B1875.G76 1990 194—dc20 90-35814
ISBN 0–19–824250–6

Typeset by Hope Services (Abingdon) Ltd
Printed and bound in
Great Britain by Biddles Ltd.
Guildford & King's Lynn

For Jules Vuillemin

Acknowledgements

ONE of the insufficiently recognized pleasures of philosophy is the chance it gives to enter into conversations that last over years. Carried on face to face, or by letter, telephone, and the exchange of papers, these conversations occupy a middle ground that touches on both friendship and professional civility. It's lucky that no one can have the last word in these sometimes dispassionate, sometimes heated exchanges, so that they can run on and on, even beyond our lifetimes. I am grateful to the people and conversations that have sustained, enriched, and revised the writing of this book.

The dedication acknowledges my first debt of gratitude, to Jules Vuillemin. He has been not only a careful and serious reader of my work, but has provided an exemplary combination of speculative philosopher and meticulous historian. His reflective assessment of important episodes in the history of logic, mathematics, and metaphysics so as to question assumptions and revive possibilities in contemporary philosophy, is an unfailing source of inspiration. I would also like to thank him and his wife Gudrun for their hospitality on a number of occasions.

I have profited immensely from the important work of Henk Bos in the history of seventeenth-century mathematics, as well as from his conversation and criticism. Daniel Garber's articles on Descartes's physics and metaphysics, and his lively and instructive talk, have likewise served as important sources for this book. The criticism, books, and translations of Marjorie Grene and Roger Ariew, my friends at VPI, have left their imprint, especially on the last chapter. Discussions with Michael Resnik and Philip Kitcher have taught me a great deal about the nature of reduction and mathematical knowledge. And John Yolton's broad understanding of seventeenth-century philosophy, enriched by his enthusiastic bibliophilia, has formed an important part of this book's background.

A rolling stone gathers no moss, but a travelling philosopher picks up lots of useful information. Edith Sylla's essays on proportion were a revelation to me when I was down in North Carolina. And in Rome, Guiseppa Battisti's work on proportion and her conversations about Descartes were invaluable. Off and on throughout the last decade in Paris, I have profited from the philosophical and historical scholarship of François De Gandt (and from his kind hospitality and that of his family.) Herbert Breger in Hanover has given me astute advice about seventeenth-century mathematics and science. Alan Gabbey and Craig Fraser in Toronto helped me revise the middle chapters of this book.

I would like to thank the National Endowment for the Humanities for their support during 1985–6, when I was a Fellow at the National Humanities Center. My gratitude to the Center itself is profound, for the time and the superb library resources it offered allowed me to draft the whole plan of this book, and write a number of its chapters. I am grateful as well to the Institute for the History and Philosophy of Science and Technology at the University of Toronto, where as a Senior Research Fellow I put the finishing touches on this manuscript during 1988–9. I would like to thank the Philosophy Department at the Pennsylvania State University, and in particular my chair, Carl Vaught, for their continuing support of my projects. Sandra Stelts and Charles Mann of the Rare Books Room of Penn State's Pattee Library were also most kind in helping me to obtain photographs of illustrations in some of the original texts, including Descartes's *Geometry* (*Geometria*, Amsterdam, 1683), *Principles of Philosophy* (*Principia Philosophiae*, Amsterdam, 1644), and *Treatise of Man* (*L'Homme*, Paris: Theodore Girard, 1664), and Isaac Newton's *Philosophiae Naturalis Principia Mathematica* (Amsterdam, 1714). Finally, I would like to thank the editors at Oxford University Press for their assistance and encouragement, and the readers for their useful suggestions about the text.

My deepest thanks go to my husband, Robert Edwards, for the example of his own scholarship and for his presence, understanding, and enthusiasm. We would both like to thank our baby boy, Benjamin, for brightening up the last stages of the production of this book.

E. R. G.

Contents

Introduction	1
1. Descartes's *Geometry* and Pappus' Problem	15
2. Treatment of Curves: Notion of Genre	38
3. Descartes's *Principles:* Physical Unities	61
4. Laws of Motion	80
5. Historical Context of Cartesian Physics	99
6. Descartes's Physiology	117
7. The *Meditations* Re-examined	133
Bibliography	153
Index	159

Introduction

DESCARTES was not only a philosopher, but a mathematician and physicist as well. Over the centuries and with currently renewed intensity, his *Meditations* has never failed to inspire serious discussion among philosophers. And Descartes himself was aware of the depth and importance of its metaphysical deduction, the chain of reasoning which exemplifies Cartesian method in a peculiarly pure way, and grounds the rest of Descartes's enterprises, mathematics, science, and the study of happiness. Yet he warns us not to concentrate too much on the *Meditations* alone; the study of nature and the human passions is just as important as the purely intellectual investigation of metaphysics.[1] To treat Descartes simply as a philosopher and to study the *Meditations* in isolation from the rest of his undertakings is thus to misunderstand him on his own terms.

Indeed, Descartes's claims about method, central to all his philosophical work, entail that none of his writings can be understood properly in isolation, but only according to its place within his system as a whole. By appending the *Geometry* to the *Discourse on Method* and by commencing the *Principles of Philosophy* with Part I, 'Of the Principles of Human Knowledge', Descartes carefully locates his mathematics and physics with respect to the argument of the *Meditations,* which is prior in the methodological 'order of reasons' and provides their metaphysical justification. By the same token, Meditation VI points to the scientific and moral enterprises it is designed to legitimize.

But contemporary debate has tended to suppress or question the centrality of Cartesian method, or to understand it merely as the 'method of doubt' in relation to epistemological considerations of truth and certainty.[2] This tendency distorts our understanding of Descartes's achievements, and also inhibits our ability to diagnose the persistent tensions within his system of thought. By contrast, I want to define Descartes's method in broader terms, in order to trace its impact on the domains of mathematics and physics as well as metaphysics. Its impact, analogous in all three domains, will prove to be both helpful and restrictive, and thus to underlie some of the important difficulties in the great thought experiment of the *Meditations.*

Descartes has a 'method' applicable to every area of human knowledge first of all because he is an intuitionist.[3] This method is not logicist, sceptical, or scientific. Rather, it performs the metaphysical function of making explicit how an object of knowledge must come to be known by a knower. Each intuitionist philosopher, Epicurus and Kant as well as Descartes, offers a canon of representation in order to criticize and correct the dogmatic assumption that metaphysics can set up a correspondence between assertions and an object given independently of any activity of the knower. The intuitionist adequation holds rather between the representation and the canonical procedure of its construction as an object of knowledge. For Descartes, the canon of constructibility is his method.[4] And this canon is prior to and independent of logic; the intuitionist mistrusts logic's propensity to set itself up as (in Kantian terms) an organon descriptive of things in themselves.[5] Intuitionist use of a canon is also critical, finitistic, and constructivist, mapping out a sphere into which human knowledge can reliably be extended, and beyond which it may not venture.

Secondly, Descartes's particular version of an intuitionist canon is reductionist.[6] Cartesian method organizes items of knowledge within a domain, and domains within the sphere of knowledge as a whole, according to an order of reasons, which begins with self-evidently indubitable, clear and distinct ideas, 'atoms of evidence', and proceeds by a chain of reasoning intended to be both truth-preserving and ampliative.[7] Each item in the linear unfolding of knowledge from 'simple', clear and distinct ideas that provide the starting-points must be understandable solely on the basis of the ideas that precede it. Thus, one must always be able to 'lead back' more esoteric, mediately known, compound, complex items to the simples from which they arise. As I will argue throughout this book, the reductionist thrust of Cartesian method, while in some ways an admirable problem-solving device, also makes it difficult for Descartes to account for the unity of complex entities, because they tend to decompose into simples, as in general his hierarchically stratified domains tend to collapse back into homogeneity. The domains constructed according to Descartes's intuitionist canon are therefore rendered unstable by his reductionism.

Another, related instability plagues the Cartesian domains. Each of them can be understood as a novel amalgamation of formerly distinct or at least very incompletely unified domains: the *Geometry* brings together geometry and algebra, the *Principles* geometry and physics, the *Treatise of Man* physics and medical physiology, and the *Meditations* mechanical philosophy and scholastic theology. As I have argued elsewhere, the unification of domains contributes to the growth of knowledge when and because it exploits partially shared structure between domains that none the less retain their autonomy and distinctness. Revelation is impaired when domains are held too far apart, or assimilated too closely.[8] But Descartes's way of constructing knowledge can produce both these unfortunate outcomes, for it tends to reduce the internal and external articulation of domains to the homogeneity of chosen starting-points. In the scientific works, he presents algebra and the realm of number as wholly subordinate to geometry, and physics and biology as conflated into a kind of kinematical geometry. As I shall argue, this misunderstanding seriously impairs the progress of his scientific programmes. By contrast, the problematic dualism of the *Meditations* is never resolved; as many scholars have argued over the years, the soul is never embodied in a satisfactory way.[9] Unfortunately, Descartes has served as a harbinger for contemporary philosophers whose view of reductive relations among domains of knowledge also degenerates into dualism or over-unification.[10]

The central importance of Descartes's reductionist canon of construction has been missed by many scholars who have rejected method as the key to interpreting Descartes's texts, or have understood it in a narrowly epistemological way, thus failing to embed his philosophical projects in the broader context of his work as a whole. Cartesian method is not just concerned with establishing certainty among deductively related propositions; it is more fundamentally committed to constructing objects of knowledge as orderly domains And that canonical construction is perennially vexed by Descartes's unexamined faith in the power of reduction.

As Descartes reveals in the *Discourse on Method*, his study of the methods of mathematics and his own early successes in that field led him to his conception of method. Thus he presupposes both that his mathematical work accurately exemplifies his method, and that its successes are due to the application of correct method. (To the extent that his physics is a kind of material geometry, he would also make the same claims for science.)[11] These successes give his method justificatory support in so far as they show it to be both truth-transmitting and ampliative.

But the *Meditations* is prior to the *Geometry* and the *Principles* because mathematics and science cannot by themselves demonstrate the objective validity of the method which constructs them. The *Meditations* is intended to provide that demonstration; it is a singularly pure application of method, tied to no specific subject-matter, for uncovering method's own warrant.[12] Analogously, in the *Critique of Pure Reason*, Kant not only points to the successful employment of synthetic a priori principles in geometry and physics to justify the need for identifying the transcendental structures of experience, but also offers a transcendental deduction of those structures, which the sciences of themselves do not provide.

Thus, the philosophical status of the *Meditations* cannot be disentangled from that of Descartes's scientific writings, for they are multiply sewn together by the *fil conducteur* of method. Mathematics, and by implication science, are alleged to be successful examples of the application of method; if they do not always exemplify this method and if indeed its impact can be shown to impair as well as to enhance their development, then the legitimacy of Cartesian method and with it the project of the *Meditations* is impugned.

Even the modern philosophers who have appreciated the significance of Descartes's method and thus speculated about the relation between his mathematics and philosophy, have not in general understood the negative, ambiguous lesson to be learned from tracing the application of method in the *Geometry*. Martial Gueroult, whose exposition of the *Meditations* in *Descartes selon l'ordre des raisons* is arguably the most important produced in the twentieth century, admits a very strong analogy between Descartes's analytic procedure in metaphysics and geometry, in order to defend the cogency of the *Meditations*.

It is impossible to contest the intertwined terms in a mathematical proof by reference to a term foreign to it, nor is it possible to suppose that in a series of reasons, each of which entails the succeeding one, the last although depending on the others, could be used to challenge the positing of those preceding it. . . . Thus philosophy is developed as a pure geometry, which owes all its certainty to the internal linkage of its reasons, without any reference to external reality.[13]

And Jules Vuillemin, in his *Mathématiques et métaphysique chez Descartes*, argues that the order of reasons in the *Meditations* is modelled on the construction of extended proportionalities in the

Introduction 5

Geometry. As Descartes's procedures in the Geometry limit the extent of geometry (too strictly, Vuillemin admits), so the argument of the *Meditations* critically limits the extent of human knowledge to ideas proportional to the 'I think' with which it begins.[14] L. J. Beck, in *The Method of Descartes*, treats the *Geometry* in some detail as an illustration of Descartes's analytic method, assessing his solution of 'Pappus' problem' and the associated classification of curves according to 'genre', as wholly successful and indeed as owing their success precisely to the application of method. He claims, 'The *Géométrie* reproduces clearly the fundamental characteristics of the analytical method and illustrates the reduction of a problem to its most general and most simple form.'[15] The treatment of the *Geometry* in Peter Schouls's *The Imposition of Method, A Study of Descartes and Locke*, is rather more cursory, but his conclusion is the same: 'method determines the techniques of a science in the sense that, in terms of geometry, the presence of method allows for a demonstration (allows for a clear exposition and hence a full understanding of the problem).'[16] With the exception of Vuillemin, whose reservations are on the whole less severe than and differently located from my own, all these commentators accept Descartes's claims for his method in its application to mathematics.

By contrast, my intention in this book is in fact to criticize Descartes's conception of method, by showing that it not only helps to organize and extend but also in important respects obfuscates and impoverishes the domains to which he applies it, even mathematics. Indeed, mathematics proves to be the crucial touchstone of his method's limitations. The ambiguous impact of reduction as an instrument of discovery and domain-building should become apparent in my novel reading of the *Geometry*, the *Principles*, and Descartes's physiological psychology in the *Treatise of Man*, and thus lead as well to a reevaluation of the *Meditations*.

The following passages from the *Discourse on Method* will serve as a point of reference and summary of Descartes's analytic method, and will further underline how crucial the evaluation of his *Geometry* is to an understanding of that method.[17]

Those long chains of reasoning, simple and easy as they are, of which geometricians make use in order to arrive at the most difficult demonstrations, had caused me to imagine that all those things which fall under the cognizance of man might very likely be mutually related in the same fashion; and that, provided only that we abstain from receiving anything as true which is not so, and always retain the order which is necessary in order to deduce the one conclusion from the other, there can be nothing so remote that we cannot reach to it, nor so recondite that we cannot discover it.

Descartes supposes that human knowledge can be organized as a rigorous chain of items of knowledge arranged according to the order of reasons, so that those laid down first must be known without the aid of those that follow, and those that follow must be so arranged that they are shown to be true solely by those that precede.[18] This passage also indicates that knowledge is a single, unbroken chain; for Descartes, the sciences are one in the strongest possible sense, not only because they all share the same method, but because method arrays them as a linearly ordered unity.

And I had not much trouble in discovering which objects it was necessary to begin with, for I already knew that it was with the most simple and those most easy to apprehend. Considering also that of all those who have hitherto sought for the truth in the Sciences, it has been the mathematicians alone who have been able to succeed in making any demonstrations, that is to say producing reasons which are evident and certain, I did not doubt that it had been by means of a similar kind that they carried on their investigations. I did not at the same time hope for any practical result in so doing, except that my mind would become accustomed to the nourishment of truth and would not content itself with false reasoning.

Descartes also characterizes the analytic order of reasons as a progression from the simple to the complex, from the atom of evidence whose objective validity is internal to it[19] to stepwise constructed, rationally articulated, systematic wholes. And he notes in passing that it is not particularly difficult to identify the simples which figure as starting-points.

But for all that I had no intention of trying to master all those particular sciences that receive in common the name of Mathematics; but observing that, although their objects are different, they do not fail to agree in this, that they take nothing under consideration but the various relationships or proportions which are present in these objects, I thought that it would be better if I only examined these proportions in their general aspect, and without viewing them otherwise than in the objects which would serve most to facilitate a knowledge of them. Not that I should in any way restrict them to these objects, for I might later on all the more easily apply them to all other objects to which they were applicable.

Introduction

Finally, Descartes indicates that he considers the abstract relational structure provided by proportions, a:b::c:d::e:f . . . , to be an accurate schema for the articulated wholes in which atoms of evidence will figure as terms. As Vuillemin points out, the mathematical theory of proportions serves as a model of Descartes's method; the step-by-step constructions of his analysis are like the construction of unknown terms in a proportion.[20] Just as the theory of proportions can be applied to any kind of mathematical object, so Cartesian method applies uniformly to all subject-matters.

The passages I have just quoted are a gloss on the four precepts of his method, which sum up the requirements of simple and evident starting-points, step-by-step construction, fidelity to the order of reasons, and completeness in the resultant complex whole.

The first of these was to accept nothing as true which I did not clearly recognize to be so: that is to say, carefully to avoid precipitation and prejudice in judgements, and to accept in them nothing more than what was presented to my mind so clearly and distinctly that I could have no occasion to doubt it.

The second was to divide up each of the difficulties which I examined into as many parts as possible, and as seemed requisite in order that it might be resolved in the best manner possible.

The third was to carry on my reflections in due order, commencing with objects that were the most simple and easy to understand, in order to rise little by little, or by degrees, to knowledge of the most complex, assuming an order, even if a fictitious one, among those which do not follow a natural sequence relatively to one another.

The last was in all cases to make enumerations so complete and reviews so general that I should be certain to have omitted nothing.[21]

The collective import of these four precepts is that Cartesian method is a powerful instrument for organizing domains of knowledge, and for aligning and unifying them. Its general tendency is to reduce, integrate, and homogenize domains. Using it, Descartes renovates metaphysics, mathematics, and science and establishes unprecedented relations among them.

Yet in so far as it can be successfully applied, this method proves a double-edged instrument that blocks as well as opens up areas of research. It suppresses important questions: What other possibilities have been excluded in the choice of simple and evident starting-points? What antecedents do the starting-points have? To what extent can the items of a domain be treated as homogeneous? To what extent do they instantiate the relational structures so far adduced to characterize them? What possibilities have been excluded in the choice of relational structure? Do distinct domains resist being assimilated to each other? What is sacrificed when complexity and heterogeneity are reduced by method? And, how can simples account for the unity of complex wholes, like curves in mathematics, material objects and vortices in physics, the human body in physiology, and the human self in philosophy?

Moreover, to the extent that Descartes believes that his method is both ampliative and truth-preserving, it cannot be successfully applied, for as such it is non-existent. Inductive methods which extend knowledge are corrigible, and deductive methods which reliably transmit truth cannot be ampliative. Thus Descartes must frequently smuggle in extra bits of knowledge to which he is not strictly entitled in order to generate his new subject-matters. And when he does not, the 'simplicity' of his starting-points impoverishes the new domain, or involves him in thorny problems of circularity.

Methods that proceed by reduction, that forget complexity in the service of problem-solving, are most plausible and successful in mathematics. And, as I have stressed, Descartes points to mathematics as the discipline that first led him to formulate his conception of method. My discussion of Cartesian method will therefore begin with the *Geometry*. Chapter 1 concerns the opening pages of Book I, and Descartes's solution to Pappus' problem. Chapter 2 investigates Descartes's treatment of curves and his notion of genre. My exposition is designed to show in detail how his method acts as a powerful problem-solving device which none the less weakens its own results and diverts Descartes from important mathematical questions which some of his contemporaries were already exploring.

Chapter 3 examines Descartes's difficulties in establishing starting-points for his physics, Chapter 4 reviews his laws of motion, and Chapter 5 compares in some detail Descartes's scientific achievements with those of his contemporaries. All three chapters explore the questions of how Descartes's mathematics, shaped by his method, interacts with his physics, and how his method bears directly on the subject-matter of the *Principles*. While Cartesian method helps generate the first cosmological and systematic physics since Aristotle's, which would dominate European thought until usurped by Newton's *Principia*, it prevents Descartes from quantifying the

Introduction

temporal and dynamic aspects of physical phenomena, and from understanding how imperfect his model of the stability of physical objects and systems really is. Chapter 6 treats the physiology, which I claim must be read as a materialist epistemology, given in the *Treatise of Man*. I show various difficulties which such a reductionist model for the acquisition of animal (or human) knowledge entails, as well as the promise and problems of the relationship between physics and biology projected by Descartes.

The materialist epistemology of the *Treatise of Man* provides an interesting foil for the theorationalist epistemology of the *Meditations*. In the final chapter I re-examine the argument of the *Meditations*, and attempt both to do justice to its coherence within its historical situation, and to reveal difficulties in its unfolding by diagnosing them as the effects of Cartesian method. My preliminary studies of the impact of this method on other subject-matters will lend my conclusions sharpness and precision, in the case where Descartes applies it reflexively to thinking. And my conclusions will be supported, as I hope, by the precautions I have taken to criticize Descartes through holding him to his own or neighbouring standards.

In my treatment of the *Meditations*, I have used as a counterpoint Martial Gueroult's *Descartes selon l'ordre des raisons* (aided by Roger Ariew's fine translation), as well as the careful and thought-provoking, but more critical arguments of Margaret Wilson, Harry Frankfurt, and Marjorie Grene. In my opinion, Gueroult has given the best apology for the *Meditations* written in the twentieth century. So I have tried not to make a straw man of Descartes, criticize his argument piecemeal, or judge him by twentieth-century standards, by keeping Gueroult's version of Descartes's argument clearly in view, even where I part company with it. The work of Wilson, Frankfurt, and Grene has likewise been instructive for, despite their criticisms, they take pains to respect the integrity of the argument of the *Meditations*.

So in a way I am sorry that this book is as negative as it is. Its negative animus is fuelled by my quarrel not only with Descartes but with certain trends in twentieth-century philosophy. I have spent much of the last decade thinking about questions of reduction, and arguing for heterogeneity and multiplicity, for unifications that are partial and piecemeal, among mathematical domains, between mathematics and physics, physics and biology, biology and the human sciences. Reduction is a powerful conceptual tool, but it becomes dangerous without a careful understanding of its limitations and origins. I think Descartes misunderstands his own reductions, and that his misunderstanding is crystallized in his method. And Descartes's position in the Western tradition is so central that his misunderstandings have remained with us.

Like the recurrent Platonism and Kantianism that both guide and skew our ways of thinking, the influence of Descartes stands in need of continually renewed criticism. As I was writing this book, I often rehearsed between the lines my opposition to the hegemony of the notion of theory in the sciences (and in the humanities, where it is even more damaging), in my view an offspring of Descartes's order of reasons, sired and logicized perhaps by Leibniz's universal characteristic. I thought of the Churchlands' 'eliminative reduction' of folk psychology (i.e. human wisdom) in favour of descriptions of neuronal states; and the milder forms of such reduction embodied in the currently popular 'naturalized epistemologies'. And I thought of Quine's claim that geometry is arithmetic and arithmetic is logic, and his penchant for ontological parsimony. Much of modern philosophy bears the traces of Descartes's reductive method, as far as I can see, and requires prolonged and deep philosophical criticism in order to make that influence visible, and so subject to further reflection. Thus despite my respect for and fascination with Descartes's work, I have written this book as a critique.

Notes

1. Descartes is recorded as making this remark in the *Entretiens avec Burman*, in Descartes, *Œuvres*, ed. C. Adam and P. Tannery (12 vols.; new edn., Paris: Vrin, 1964–74, v. 165. Hereafter I will refer to this edition as AT, followed by volume and page number.
2. D. Garber e.g. argues that considerations of method cease to be important in the works of Descartes's mature period, in his essay 'Descartes et la Méthode en 1637' in N. Grimaldi and J.-L. Marion (eds.), *Le Discours et sa Méthode* (Paris: Presses Universitaires de France, 1987), 65–87. Garber argues that method, as enunciated in the *Rules* and applied in the *Optics* and *Meteorology* is primarily a device for solving individual problems. While I agree with him on this point, and on the further point that the synthetic moment of the method fades away, I see Descartes not as losing interest in method altogether during the crucial period of the early 1630s, but rather as coming to understand it as a way of organizing whole subject-matters according to the analytic order of reasons.

    Despite the fine analyses of particular arguments offered by M. Wilson in *Descartes* (The Arguments of the Philosophers Series; London: Routledge & Kegan Paul, 1978), she suppresses the question of method altogether. And H. Frankfurt discusses method only in terms of the method of doubt, which however he subjects to penetrating analysis in *Demons, Dreamers and Madmen: The Defense of Reason in Descartes's Meditations* (The History of Philosophy Series; Indianapolis and New York: Bobbs-Merrill, 1970).
3. I use this term in a general metaphysical sense suggested by J. Vuillemin in *Nécessité ou contingence: L'aporie de Diodore et les systèmes philosophiques* (Paris: Éditions de Minuit, 1984), 189–229 and 357–406, as well as in *What are Philosophical Systems?* (Cambridge: Cambridge University Press, 1986). Vuillemin proposes a classification of metaphysical systems derived from a classification of judgements, of which intuitionism is one.
4. Since Descartes is an intuitionist in this sense, he cannot espouse a correspondence theory of truth, as Frankfurt points out in *Demons, Dreamers and Madmen*. But his position does not for that reason amount merely to a coherence theory of truth, for ideas are always for him representations and at least one of them (the idea of God) so far transcends his powers of construction that it demonstrates the existence of what it represents independent of the knower.
5. Thus Y. Belaval opposes Descartes the intuitionist to Leibniz the

formalist and logician in *Leibniz critique de Descartes* (Paris: Gallimard, 1960). See also I. Hacking's 'Proof and Eternal Truths: Descartes and Leibniz' in S. Gaukroger (ed.), *Descartes: Philosophy, Mathematics and Physics* (Brighton: Harvester Press, 1980), 169–80. Descartes is thoroughly distrustful of the formal apparatus of logic.

6. There are many ways to define reduction. In a broad, informal sense, it is a habit of thought for dealing with complex situations by forgetting some structure in order to arrive at a more manageable and yet still significant remnant. Its advantage is conceptual streamlining; its disadvantage is forgetfulness. In group theory e.g. one often investigates a complex, perhaps infinitary group by 'modding out' a subgroup and then dealing with the simpler group of equivalence classes thereby formed. In algebraic topology, one treats curved spaces (manifolds) as locally, though not globally, reducible to flat, Euclidean spaces. In analysis, the integration of an unpleasant function can under certain circumstances be reduced to integrating a sum or product or series of more tractable functions. As these examples show, reductions may be carried out on objects or problems, and may be expressed as generalizable procedures.

In recent philosophical literature, reduction is often discussed as a relation holding between theories couched in a suitable formal language. For typical examples, see E. Nagel, *The Structure of Science* (New York: Harcourt, Brace & World, 1961), esp. ch. 11, and D. Bonevac, *Reduction in the Abstract Sciences* (Cambridge, Mass.: Hackett Publishing Co., 1982). On this account, one theory reduces to another if, once its vocabulary has been translated into the vocabulary of the reducing theory, it can be derived as a set of theorems from the axioms of the reducing theory. Subsequent discussion has questioned whether the notion of theory adequately characterizes areas of scientific research and whether the relations between such areas are captured by such a narrow and logicized sense of reduction. See e.g. the arguments put forward by D. Shapere in 'Scientific Theories and their Domains' in F. Suppe (ed.), *The Structure of Scientific Theories* (Urbana: University of Illinois Press, 1974), 518–65 and by N. Maull and L. Darden, in 'Interfield Theories' in *Philosophy of Science*, 44 (1977), 43–64, apropos the first issue; and those by L. Sklar in 'Types of Inter-Theoretic Reduction' in the *British Journal for Philosophy of Science*, 18 (1967), 109–24, by T. Nickles in 'Theory Generalization, Problem Reduction and the Unity of Science' in R. S. Cohen *et al.* (eds.), *PSA 1974* (Dordrecht: D. Reidel, 1976), 33–75, and by N. Maull in 'Unifying Science Without Reduction' in *Studies in the History and Philosophy of Science*, 8 (1977), 143–62, apropos the second.

In general, I prefer to use the richer notion of 'domain' proposed by

Introduction 13

Shapere, which includes characteristic objects, problems, techniques, and styles of justification as well as, possibly, a formalized theory, to refer to areas of scientific research. And I am certainly convinced that relations among domains are far more interesting and indeterminate than logical derivation, even though I appreciate the illumination of some aspects of reduction offered by the notion of a formal theory. In particular, I think it would be inappropriate and anachronistic in this book to analyse Descartes's way of unifying the sciences according to the narrowly logicist sense of reduction. So I introduce the term in the vaguer and broader sense given at the beginning of this note, and trust that the exposition of method in the following chapters will adequately clarify its meaning.

7. The locution 'atoms of evidence' is borrowed from J.-L. Marion, *Sur l'ontologie grise de Descartes* (Paris: Vrin, 1975), 135. Descartes distinguishes between analytic and synthetic order at the end of the *Second Replies*, AT vii. 155–6, but, I would argue, in his later works the synthetic procedure is suppressed. The argument of the *Geometry*, the parts of the *Principles* I discuss in detail, and the *Meditations* are thus structured according to the analytic order of reasons. For a discussion of this distinction, see M. Gueroult, *Descartes selon l'ordre des raisons* (2 vols.; Paris: Aubier, Éditions Montaigne, 1968), i. 22–3, trans. R. Ariew, *Descartes' Philosophy Interpreted According to the Order of Reasons* (2 vols.; Minneapolis: University of Minnesota Press, 1984), i. 7–8. Peter Schouls, in *The Imposition of Method: A Study of Descartes and Locke* (Oxford: Clarendon Press, 1980), 15–21, discusses the distinction, and D. Garber and L. Cohen in 'A Point of Order: Analysis, Synthesis and Descartes's *Principles*' in *Archiv für Geschichte der Philosophie*, 64 (1982), 136–47, argue that the *Principles* is not written in the synthetic mode.

8. I argue this position in 'Wittgenstein and the Correlation of Logic and Arithmetic', *Ratio*, 23 (1981), 31–42; 'Leibniz's Unification of Geometry with Algebra and Dynamics', *Studia Leibnitiana* Special Issue 13 (1984), 198–208; 'Two Episodes in the Unification of Logic and Topology', *British Journal for the Philosophy of Science*, 36 (1985), 147–57; and 'Some Uses of Proportion in Newton's *Principia*, bk. I: A Case Study in Applied Mathematics', *Studies in the History and Philosophy of Science*, 18 (1987), 209–20.

9. A trenchant reprise of this theme is given by M. Grene in her *Descartes* (Philosophers in Context; Minneapolis: University of Minnesota Press, 1985), esp. ch. 2.

10. Apropos an attempted reduction of mathematics to logic, see W. V. O. Quine, *From a Logical Point of View* (New York: Harper & Row, 1963) and C. Chihara, *Ontology and the Vicious Circle Principle*

(Ithaca: Cornell University Press, 1973). Apropos an attempted reduction of mind to brain activity, see P. Churchland, *Matter and Consciousness* (Cambridge, Mass.: MIT Press, 1988) and R. G. Millikan, *Language, Thought and Other Biological Categories* (Cambridge, Mass.: MIT Press, 1984). A milder version of the latter reduction underlies A. Goldman, *Epistemology and Cognition* (Cambridge, Mass.: Harvard University Press, 1986).
11. G. Hatfield argues that Descartes did not understand the micromechanisms proposed in the *Principles* to be part of the order of reasons in 'Science, Certainty and Descartes', *PSA 1988*, 2 (East Lansing: Philosophy of Science Association, 1989). I think it may be debated how Descartes understood the relation between the microscopic and in principle mathematizable phenomena proposed in his physics, and the macroscopic (sensible and empirical) phenomena of free fall, projectile motion, and simple machines; he may well have hoped that science would one day bridge and thus rationalize and mathematize the gap. In any case, the picture of Descartes as an empiricist in D. Clarke, *Descartes' Philosophy of Science* (University Park: Pennsylvania State University Press, 1982) seems to me, while provocative of useful debate, too extreme.
12. Gueroult, *Descartes selon l'ordre des raisons*, i. 86–94; Ariew, *Descartes' Philosophy*, i. 52–7.
13. Gueroult, *Descartes selon l'ordre des raisons*, i. 21–2; Ariew, *Descartes' Philosophy*, i. 6–7.
14. *Mathématiques et métaphysique chez Descartes* (Paris: Presses Universitaires de France, 1960), ch. 4.
15. *The Method of Descartes* (Oxford: Oxford University Press, 1952), 185.
16. Schouls, *Imposition of Method*, p. 73.
17. *Discours de la Méthode*, AT vi. 19–20. The translation is in Descartes, *The Philosophical Works of Descartes*, ed. E. S. Haldane and G. R. T. Ross (2 vols.; Cambridge: Cambridge University Press, 1967), i. 92–3. For each citation, I will give the volume and page number in Haldane and Ross (HR), followed by the volume and page number in Adam and Tannery.
18. *Secundae Responsiones*, HR ii. 48; AT, vii. 155.
19. Gueroult, *Descartes selon l'ordre des raisons*, i. 331–7; Ariew, *Descartes' Philosophy*, i. 237–41. See also, M. Grene, *Descartes*, pp. 56–60.
20. *Mathématiques et métaphysique chez Descartes*, pp. 119–27.
21. *Discours de la Méthode*, HR i. 92; AT vi. 18–19.

1
Descartes's *Geometry* and Pappus' Problem

DESCARTES in his mature work organizes a subject-matter as a linear progression from simples to complexes, according to the order of reasons, such that each item in the chain is known without the aid of succeeding items and all items are known solely on the basis of those that precede them. Thus a domain of human knowledge will arise from starting-points which are known in themselves and develop as a progression of successively more complex entities which are simples in some kind of association. A domain thus organized, Descartes believes, will not stray beyond the boundaries of our constructive intuition and can indeed lay claim to completeness. As I showed in the Introduction, Descartes and many of his commentators take his mathematical work to exemplify and vindicate this vision of method.

But what does this picture of an organized domain amount to exactly when Cartesian method reorganizes mathematics? In the next two chapters I will take issue with the dominant account of the relation of the method to the *Geometry*. While I will try to clarify the method's power to reshape and synthesize mathematical domains, I will also criticize its reductive tendency to check the growth of knowledge and obfuscate its own successes. The passages from the *Discourse on Method* examined above continue with explicit reference to mathematics, and serve to introduce Descartes's way of thinking about the restructuring of geometry according to the order of reasons. Having noted the success of mathematics in producing 'demonstrations', Descartes goes on to say,

I had no intention of trying to master all those particular sciences that receive in common the name of mathematics; but observing that, although their objects are different, they do not fail to agree in this, that they take nothing under consideration but the various relationships or proportions which are present in these objects, I thought that it would be better if I only examined these proportions in their general aspect, and without viewing them otherwise than in the objects which would serve most to facilitate a knowledge of them. Not that I should in any way restrict them to these objects, for I might later on all the more easily apply them to all other objects to which they were applicable. Then, having carefully noted that in order to comprehend the proportions I should sometimes require to consider each one in particular, and sometimes merely keep them in mind, or take them in groups, I thought that, in order the better to consider them in detail, I should picture them in the form of lines, because I could find no method more simple nor more capable of being distinctly represented to my imagination and senses. I considered, however, that in order to keep them in my memory or to embrace several at once, it would be essential that I should explain them by means of certain formulas, the shorter the better. And for this purpose it was requisite that I should borrow all that is best in Geometrical Analysis and Algebra, and correct the errors of the one by the other.[1]

The simples for Cartesian mathematics will be straight line segments, and their form of association, proportions. The complexes will be problems and higher algebraic curves, both kinds of entities hierarchically ordered, and representable by algebraic equations.

Descartes has claimed that the starting-points in the constitution of a subject-matter are not difficult to find: 'And I had not much trouble in discovering which objects it was necessary to begin with, for I already knew that it was with the most simple and those most easy to comprehend.'[2] Descartes's choice of straight line segments as his starting-point streamlines and reorganizes parts of classical geometry in important ways. But his methodological claim suggests that he need not discuss that choice and his reasons for it, nor invoke the mathematical tradition which forms the background against which his choice is made. His starting-points therefore do not require a logos which would establish their relation to an inferential nexus or a historical tradition that looms behind them. Cartesian beginnings are supposed to be radical, justified only by the piercing vision and uninflected assent of intuition. Thus, the opening of the *Geometry* hides without comment a number of important debts and exclusions.

Descartes also claims that a whole subject-matter can be elaborated out of starting-points which are simple and easy to understand, for he believes his method to be both truth-preserving and ampliative. The *Geometry* does indeed extend the field of geometry in certain important ways. But since a procedure which is both truth-preserving and ampliative is a chimera, in so far as Descartes develops geometry from simplified beginnings he impoverishes it, and in so far as he extends it he must bring in extra assumptions without acknowledging them. So too Descartes's habit of precipitous (and often erroneous) generalization originates here. The assumption that a subject-matter can be elaborated out of self-evident and simple starting-points often involves Descartes in problems of circularity, which cluster around his notion of the pointwise constructibility of curves. The possibility that some mathematical item, X, is a starting-point, for example, will prove to require the prior availability of another item, Y; but Y was supposed to intervene later on in the 'order of reasons' as a complex construction on the basis of X. (Or Y may be one of the unacknowledged items excluded by Descartes's selection of starting-points.) Similarly, the further construction of another item, Z, out of the system at a certain stage will turn out to require W, but the availability of W cannot be guaranteed by the starting-points or by the stipulated processes of construction from them.

Finally, according to Descartes, everything important about a subject-matter can be captured in an abstract relational system, transparent to reason, whose terms are mere place-holders without intrinsic interest. Terms must therefore be homogeneous in a strong sense, for interesting heterogeneity in the terms might require an adjustment of the relational structure. Thus, Cartesian method is powerfully reductive and integrative. It allows for the forgetting of some of the complexity of classical geometry (including the idiosyncratic unity or integrity of its items) in the service of problem-solving. And it allows for differences to be forgotten in the service of unifying distinct subject-matters (geometry and the algebra of arithmetic) on the basis of similarities in their structural relations, which may in turn be a powerful problem-solving device. At the same time, this tenet impoverishes geometry by homogenizing its items, and insisting that it include nothing beyond what the relational network captures. It tends to conflate the already flattened subject-matter of geometry with that of number, in an identity which suppresses one or the other.

Moreover, abstract relations as Descartes uses them, are not only for representing relations among and therefore problems about the simplest, initial items (straight line segments) but also for constructing more complex geometrical items. These complexes, higher algebraic curves for example, having become objects of mathematical investigation in their own right, may then exhibit certain idiosyncrasies and opacities, and prove to be not entirely derivable from the simples and the alleged process of construction. In so far as Descartes wishes to insist on their derivability, the distinctions he needs for establishing a hierarchy of curves become untenable, so that the whole edifice collapses back to the simples. Abstract relations are not entirely transparent to reason and the demand for articulated hierarchy remains unresolved.

Cartesian method can be appreciated for its power to align and clarify subject-matters. Part of my intention in this chapter is to exhibit the source of Descartes's great inventive genius in the *Geometry* where he reorders and brings together geometry and algebra, thereby transforming the mathematical landscape of the seventeenth century. None the less, his method can choke and divert the growth of knowledge. When a reduction is taken as a complete expression of the whole, and a unification engulfs and collapses one of its relata, then discovery slides to a halt. Although Descartes's method is genuinely a means of discovery, it also interferes with the very developments it makes possible.

THE FIRST SEVEN PAGES OF THE *GEOMETRY*

The beginning of Descartes's *Geometry* forms a striking contrast with the beginning of Euclid's *Elements,* to which it is so thoroughly indebted. Euclid starts off his attempt to organize the field of geometry with a series of definitions, postulates, and common notions which characterize the kind of things geometry treats: points, lines, shaped surfaces, angles, triangles, and other kinds of polygons. Points, lines, and surfaces are emphatically different kinds of things. While points serve as boundaries for lines, and lines for areas, points do not compose lines, nor lines areas; higher dimensional objects cannot be reduced to the lower dimensional objects.[3]

The definition of each object underlines its differences from the others by exhibiting its peculiar kind of unity. The unity of a point is perfect but trivial, since it has no parts. As such, it neither exploits nor exhibits the extendedness of space; its unity has nothing to do with spatiality. The unity of a line is measurable, and the line serves as its own measure. The unity of a shaped surface, like a triangle, is a rich source for further investigations, both because it is so much more than the sum of its parts (lines and angles) and because it exhibits so profoundly the properties of the ambient space.

In other words, Euclid chooses as his starting-point the kinds of things which his geometry treats and gives an exposition of them before he moves on to anything else. His subject-matter has a suggestive heterogeneity which he underlines and articulates by the extended accounts provided in the complementary definitions and postulates. These accounts are explanations and exhibitions of, and leading speculations about, the kinds of unity characterizing the abstract objects of geometry.[4] Once he has given them, we can already see how the ways in which surfaces are bounded in two-dimensional space could be an endlessly interesting subject-matter, and begin to wonder about how volumes are bounded in three-dimensional space.

By contrast, Descartes opens the *Geometry* with the announcement, 'Any problem in geometry can easily be reduced to such terms that a knowledge of the lengths of certain straight lines is sufficient for its construction.'[5] With this sentence, he stipulates that geometry begins with one kind of thing, straight line segments. His second sentence tells us that all that is important about these objects is a relational structure which they share with the objects of arithmetic:

Just as arithmetic consists of only four or five operations, namely, addition, subtraction, multiplication, division and the extraction of roots, which may be considered a kind of division, so in geometry, to find required lines it is merely necessary to add or subtract other lines; or else, taking one line which I shall call unity in order to relate it as closely as possible to numbers, and which can in general be chosen arbitrarily, and having given two other lines, to find a fourth line which shall be to one of the given lines as the other is to unity (which is the same as multiplication); or, again, to find a fourth line which is to one of the given lines as unity is to the other (which is equivalent to division); or, finally, to find one, two, or several mean proportionals between unity and some other line (which is the same as extracting the square root, cube root, etc., of the given line.)[6]

Descartes has nothing to say about the context of his choice of straight line segments, what other items they exclude or presuppose, nor about their intrinsic character. As he observes in the passage from the *Discourse on Method* quoted earlier, the choice of starting-points involves no difficulty worth discussing; one chooses items which are the 'simplest and easiest to know'. Here one of the features of Descartes's intuitionism which so troubled Leibniz arises: whatever is apparent to intuition does not require an explanatory account.[7] All Descartes tells us about straight line segments is that he chose them precisely because they could serve as general objects whose idiosyncrasies, if they had any, would not intrude on his study. Though different subject-matters have different kinds of objects, he is only interested in 'the various relations or proportions subsisting among those objects'. Straight line segments are therefore to become a strangely colourless and thoroughly homogeneous subject-matter with no inherent texture of its own, which only serves to instantiate a relational structure.

Thus Descartes never mentions what he is surely well aware of, that his choice excludes the possibility of setting up ratios and proportions involving terms which are areas, curves, or infinitesimal magnitudes (which may in turn be lines, areas, and so forth). This is a serious omission, for it is with just such a rich mixture of terms that contemporary Italians, for example, are working up a geometry apt for representing physical problems which in turn suggest techniques of integration and differentiation. The diagrams which Galileo uses in the Third Day of his *Two New Sciences*[8] to analyse free fall involve infinitesimal areas, and his treatment of the Mean-Speed Theorem in other documents[9] hinges on a ratio whose terms are infinite sums of infinitesimals, 'instantaneous velocities'. Such reasonings would not have been permitted in Descartes's *Geometry*. In a sense, the first two sentences of the *Geometry* explain why Descartes was never very good at quantifying physics.

There is an obvious reason why Descartes chooses straight line segments as the subject-matter of his geometry, that is, as the terms which can appear in ratios and proportions. Since his algebra is the algebra of arithmetic, and his treatment of proportions derives from the medieval tradition which treats terms and ratios as numbers, he needs geometric items which can stand as proxies for numbers, and line segments are the likeliest candidates.[10] Points do not have the requisite variability, surfaces extend in too many directions, angles are curiously incomplete, and curves are too difficult to measure because they cannot measure themselves. Descartes never explains this, just as he never examines the peculiar kind of integrity that line segments have which in fact allows them to be the likeliest analogue to numbers.

Descartes thus gives a startlingly minimal account of his starting-points. His method says, start with what is simple and easy to understand, that is, what intuition can and must assent to. Not only is nothing required to supplement or justify intuitions's assent, but the philosopher who proceeds thus methodically need not worry that some obscurity or incompleteness in the starting-points will generate difficulties for the elaboration of the subject-matter later on. (This assumption is just what Leibniz contests.)

The éclat of Descartes's commencement of the *Geometry* is rather blinding, for it is indeed a brilliant moment of mathematical invention. The classical insistence on the heterogeneity of the objects of geometry had also impaired the possibility of certain kinds of generalization. In Greek mathematics, lines could be added and subtracted, for example, but if two lines were multiplied, they produced an area, while three lines multiplied produced a volume. Thus clearly the product of four lines could be given no comprehensible interpretation. Descartes provides a way to understand division, multiplication, and extraction of roots in a geometrical context as closed operations, which applied to line lengths would again produce line lengths. This is a very great conceptual advance, which allows for the unification and generalization of many problems in the classical Greek canon.

But Descartes's assumption of the homogeneity of his starting-points and their subordination to a relational structure, as well as their simplicity, which obviates the demand for an account of their peculiar unity, leads him to misrepresent the nature of his project in certain essential respects which will indeed prove troublesome in the long run. Thus he does not present his algebra of line lengths as the basis for an analogy between numbers and geometric entities, but as a relational structure which captures all there is to know about place-holders, line lengths whose own geometrical unity, spatiality, and geometrical context (like that given by Euclid's *Elements*) is of no importance. So he never admits to the richly heterogeneous geometrical context which he excludes, presupposes, and makes use of; he never examines a potential heterogeneity, between rational-algebraic and transcendental magnitudes, which remains even in his starkly reduced field of line lengths precisely because they have been brought into analogy with numbers; and he never worries about the differences (and similarities!) between numbers and geometrical entities which might not be captured by the common abstract structure that binds them.

22   Descartes's Geometry and Pappus' Problem

The alleged priority of Descartes's starting-points conceals not only his debt to classical geometry and his blindness to contemporary developments, but also an ineluctable circularity within his project as stated in the *Geometry*. Curved lines are not allowed to stand as terms in the ratios and proportions of the *Geometry,* only straight line segments. And yet curves are the explicit object of study in Book II of the *Geometry.* Given Descartes's statement of his method, the introduction of curves must be posterior to that of line segments; curves are constructed as complex proportions (converted into equations) holding among line segments, their terms. Yet, as we shall see, the process of construction itself requires the prior availability of curves. In sum, Descartes creates very knotty problems of justification for himself which he cannot resolve, due to his conception of method. And this is true even though his method leads him to genuine discoveries.

The two paragraphs which follow the introductory passages from the *Geometry* just quoted will illustrate my point in fairly elementary terms, and then I will go on to rather more complicated illustrations from the heart of the text. Both these paragraphs are accompanied by diagrams which are quite revealing.

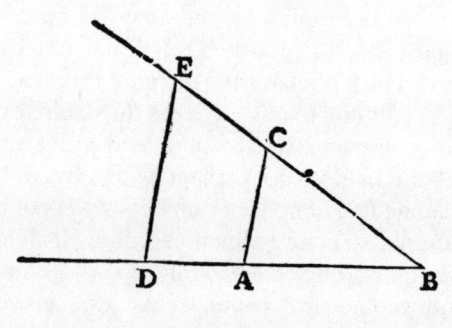

Fig. 1.1

The first is Descartes's exposition of multiplication and division (Fig. 1.1). 'For example, let AB be taken as unity, and let it be required to multiply BD by BC. I have only to join the points A and C, and draw DE parallel to CA; then BE is the product of BD and BC. If it be required to divide BE by BD, I join E and D, and draw AC parallel to DE; then BC is the result of the division.'[11] Evidently, Descartes is here setting up two proportions, AB : BD :: BC : BE and BE : BD :: BC : AB, where AB=1. Notice that the assumptions of Descartes's algebra of line lengths entail that ratios are quotients, and proportions are equivalent to equations, so that the product of the second and third terms is automatically equal to the product of the first and fourth.[12] Notice too that the proportions are justified by the construction of two similar triangles. The relationship of similarity between two triangles with the same shape is introduced in the *Elements* where it exhibits the peculiar unity of triangles.[13] Similarity of shape is a kind of integrity which no analysis of points, lines, angles or, for that matter, numbers can ever yield; a triangle is something more than the sum of its parts and is a spatial unity.

Thus apparently a knowledge of line lengths is not sufficient for an understanding of how line lengths can be associated in a construction so that they yield a product which properly mimics arithmetic. Descartes must assume as well a knowledge of triangles and the kind of unity they have which makes the equivalence relation of similarity possible. This he borrows from Euclid without acknowledging where it comes from, nor that it is not contained within the simple and easy starting-points he has proposed. Given the kinds of problems which occupy the *Geometry*, Descartes has little interest in the ways in which straight (or curved) lines enclose surfaces. We are lucky that his successors did not share this disinterest, for it blocks out, among other things, problems of integration and the founding puzzles of topology, which engaged Leibniz a generation later. Triangles are not the kind of thing that interested Descartes, nor do his starting-points entitle him to use them; but when he needs them, he borrows them from the tradition.

The following paragraph concerns the determination of square roots (see Fig. 1.2). 'If the square root of GH is desired, I add, along the same straight line, FG equal to unity; then, bisecting FH at K, I describe the circle FIH about K as a centre, and draw from G a perpendicular and extend it to I, and GI is the required root. I do not speak here of cube root, or other roots, since I shall speak more conveniently of them later.'[14] The construction of the square root requires a curve, a circle, and the construction of other roots will require other curves of higher degree. To get all the line segments which he needs as proxies for numbers, Descartes requires antecedently available curves to serve as means of construction. But Descartes wishes curves to be introduced as complex constructions

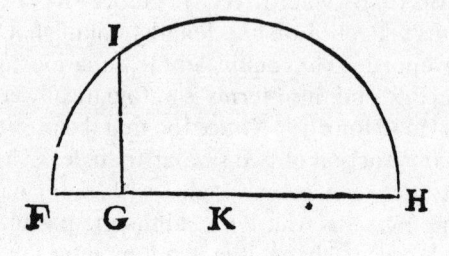

Fig. 1.2

derived from proportions holding among line segments, and does not wish to admit them as starting-points. Nor, of course, does he furnish an account of them as starting-points. Indeed, as we shall see, Descartes is really very little interested in curves.

The centrepiece of the *Geometry* is Descartes's solution to Pappus' problem, which I will discuss at length in the following section. Closely related to this problem, and somewhat more straightforward to explain, are problems which Descartes takes from the classical canon which require finding mean proportionals or dividing angles into equal parts. Descartes recasts the conditions of the problem in terms of an algebraic equation in one unknown, and then searches for the simplest curves with which to construct the roots of the equation. In the first pages of Book I he presents an equation which might represent, for example, the finding of one mean proportional between two magnitudes, or the bisecting of an angle: $z^2 = az + b^2$.[15] How does one construct the root for this equation? Descartes presents a diagram (Fig. 1.3). 'I construct a right triangle NLM with

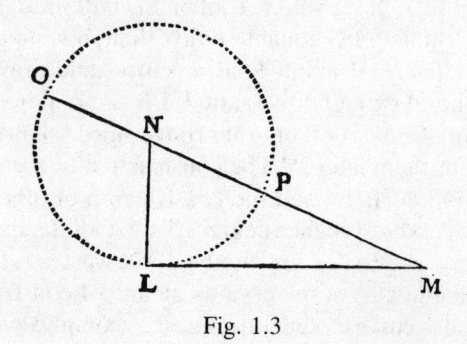

Fig. 1.3

Descartes's Geometry and Pappus' Problem

one side LM, equal to b, the square root of the known quantity b^2, and the other side, LN, equal to $\frac{1}{2}a$, that is, to half the other known quantity which we multiplied by z, which I supposed to be the unknown line. Then prolonging MN, the hypotenuse of this triangle, to O, so that NO is equal to NL, the whole line OM is the required line z. This is expressed in the following way: $z = \frac{1}{2}a + \sqrt{(\frac{1}{4}a^2 + b^2)}$.'
The construction depends on the availability of a curve, the circle, and on the Pythagorean Theorem. The latter is a stunning example in the *Elements*[16] of the interdependencies among parts that characterize the unity of those triangles which include the privileged angle, the right; again, Descartes brings this result in when he needs to, although nothing in his exposition up to that point has alluded to it.

Despite Descartes's misleading exposition, this little problem is a nice example of the great virtue of Descartes's method. Because it allows the combination of two distinct subject-matters in virtue of a common relational structure, it increases the problem-solving resources which can be brought to bear on a given problem. In this case, an originally geometrical problem can be viewed as both geometrical and algebraic, once its conditions have been reformulated as an equation. Then the algebraic formulation of the (positive) root of the equation can be applied, to suggest the geometrical configuration given above which in turn exploits the Pythagorean Theorem and the definition of the circle.

So Descartes's method brings great gains as well as a narrowing and restricting of the mathematician's attention. The three instances I have just discussed from the beginning of the *Geometry* may seem trivial, but the tendencies they illustrate pervade the whole book. In the following sections, I will discuss Descartes's larger projects in the *Geometry* of exhibiting a full solution to Pappus' problem and providing a classification of curves (which oddly transmutes into a classification of problems), and try to show that similar advantages and difficulties arise there as well.

DESCARTES'S SOLUTION TO PAPPUS' PROBLEM

Descartes understood his *Geometry* as the rationalization of classical geometry, reorganizing, pruning, and extending it by means of his new method. His method is designed to rearrange the subject-matter of geometry according to the 'order of reasons', as we have seen, so that one begins with starting-points which are simple and easy to understand, and proceeds thence step by step to construct items of increasing complexity. Thus Descartes construes his project as both conservative and revolutionary. On the one hand, he is reordering and completing an already existing domain, not founding a new one. On the other hand, the only starting-points he acknowledges are those furnished by intuition, straight line segments standing in certain relations of proportionality. His method, presupposing the radically self-grounding power of intuition, entails that his starting-points have no relation worth discussing to the tradition, nor to any inferential nexus of background knowledge in which they might be embedded. The first part of this chapter has shown how Descartes covers over his debt to the classical tradition in the very first pages of the *Geometry*.

The three famous problems of classical antiquity were the squaring of the circle, the duplication of the cube, and the trisection of the angle; much of the most interesting mathematics in antiquity was generated by the futile attempt to solve these problems with ruler and compass, and the elaboration of alternative but still (by contemporary standards) illicit means of solution. The mathematician Hippias, who taught in Athens in the second half of the fifth century BC, is best remembered for his discovery of the transcendental curve called the trisectrix or quadratrix. This curve is generated by the composition of a rotating and a translational motion, and provides easy solutions for the trisection of an angle and the squaring of a circle, when it is used as a constructing curve.[17] And Menaechmus, a student of Eudoxus who was in turn a student of Plato, discovered a whole new family of curves, the conic sections, in an attempt to solve the duplication of the cube. This problem is easily solved when two parabolas, or a rectangular hyperbola and a parabola, are used as constructing curves. The great, second century BC mathematician Archimedes developed the (transcendental) spiral named after him as a constructing curve for the trisection of the angle. Like the quadratrix, it can also be used to square the circle.[18]

Thus, the range of curves with which the Greeks were familiar was very limited; it included the straight line, the circle, the conic sections, a few isolated transcendental curves, and little else besides. In part, this was because the Greeks tended to regard curves not so much as the source or focus of problems—what problems are about—but rather as technical means for solving problems. Curves

Descartes's Geometry and Pappus' Problem 27

for the Greeks were in the first instance constructing curves. And this habit was due in turn, I think, to the relative intractability of curves for them. The Greeks had no flexible, powerful, multivalent ways of representing curves which would yield a purchase on their exploration, and therefore had no motivation to make them the centre of a research programme. The most sophisticated techniques of the age, those of 'geometrical algebra' (the application of areas and similar analytic tools) and of Archimedean quadrature, are suited for the representation and exploration not of curves, but of shaped areas.

In hindsight, we might think at first that Descartes's *Geometry* provides precisely the means of representing curves needed to bring them to the centre of the mathematical stage and make them the subject of investigation. Fermat, Descartes's rival, and Leibniz, his respectfully dissenting student, both recognize and exploit the powerful means furnished by analytic geometry for representing curves as geometric-algebraic-numerical hybrids which are simultaneously spatially shaped configurations, algebraic equations in two unknowns, and an infinite array of number pairs.

Descartes however never clearly understands this consequence of his work. His method leaves him unable to focus attention on the study of curves as such; sharing this limitation of perspective with the Greeks, he is also unable to expand the collection of curves much beyond the classical canon. My contention is that for Descartes the subject-matter of geometry always tends to revert to straight line segments and the relations of proportionality in which they stand. The demands of his method are so strongly reductive that any other possible object of investigation is either excluded or disintegrated.

The novel integrity of curves *qua* geometric-algebraic-numerical hybrids is constituted by their shape on the one hand, and on the other by the way in which they set up functional interdependencies among the parameters associated with them (ordinate, abscissa, arc length, radius, polar arc, normal, area between curve and the x-axis, circumscribed rectangle, tangent, subtangent, and so forth). Descartes never sees the potential of this new kind of mathematical unity. Throughout the *Geometry*, he rarely bothers to sketch a curve, and when he does so it is in fragmentary and sometimes erroneous fashion. To put this in slightly different terms, Descartes mentions the fact that curves correspond to indeterminate algebraic equations in two unknowns only incidentally and not very clearly in the middle of Book II of the *Geometry*.[19] And while Descartes also mentions in passing in Book II that his method of relating the points of a curve to the points of a straight line can help in determining 'its diameters, axes, centre and other lines or points which have especial significance for the curve' as well as the magnitudes of areas pertinent to quadrature, the forerunner of integration, this observation is only peripheral to the real concerns of the rest of the book.[20] He spends most of the *Geometry* studying determinate algebraic equations in one unknown which represent problems like the trisection of the angle. For him, this means constructing ordinates for given abscissas, that is, constructing further line segments on the basis of a given configuration of line segments.

The contrast with Fermat here is striking. As is well known, Fermat was developing what was to become analytic geometry concurrently with Descartes, and his introductory exposition of it is to be found in his *Ad locus planos et solidos isagoge*.[21] Fermat immediately makes the analogy of number and geometrical items explicit because he emphasizes the sketching of indeterminate equations in two variables, whereas Descartes begins and ends his book with the geometrical construction of the roots of determinate equations in one variable, that is, again, the construction of a new line segment on the basis of a given nexus of line segments.

Fermat starts off his exposition by sketching the simplest case of a linear equation, $ax = by$, and showing that it is always a straight line; thus, he says, every equation (in two variables) of first degree represents a straight line. He then goes on to give a comprehensive account of the various cases of quadratic equations in two unknowns, and the curves with which they are correlated. For the most part, he chooses his line of ordinates at right angles to the line of abscissas (a sign that he is thinking of the axes as given prior to any geometric configuration); and he investigates how to simplify the form of equations by rotating and translating axes. In other words, Fermat is centrally interested in curves, and presents them in such a way that their dual nature, as both spatial, shaped configurations, and algebraic-arithmetic formulae, is foremost.

Descartes's reductive method, however, prevents him from appreciating the integrity of curves because it disintegrates them by the very means which allows them to become objects of study. My contention naturally raises the question, what then is going on in

Book II of the *Geometry* where according to the section headings, Descartes is investigating and classifying curves? In the next chapter, I will show that Descartes's primary interest in the *Geometry* is the classification of problems (articulated as determinate equations in one unknown), that he undertakes the classification of curves only in order to enhance his classification of problems, and that indeed sometimes he seems to confuse the two kinds of classification, as if classifying problems took care of the classification of curves.

But an account of Descartes's classificatory scheme must begin with a description of Pappus' problem. Pappus of Alexandria flourished in the fourth century AD; in Book VII of his *Collection* he went beyond the two classical strategies for generating new curves, kinematic superposition, and conic sections, in a significant fashion.[22] There he proposed a generalization of a problem which had been around since Euclid, and which implied a whole new class of curves. Descartes has the great insight to take this problem up again and make it the centrepiece of the *Geometry*. Since it was a problem which the Greek mathematicians could formulate, but not solve in a systematic way nor properly generalize, it exhibits nicely the power of Cartesian method. And it also fits his method's picture of what a geometrical problem should look like, for it involves proportions whose terms are certain finite rectilinear line segments.

In brief, Pappus' problem asks for the determination of a locus whose points satisfy one of the following conditions illustrated by Fig. 1.4. Let the d_i denote the length of the line segment from point P to L_i which makes an angle of ϕ_i with L_i. Choose α/β to be a given ratio and a to be a given line segment.

The problem is to find the points P which satisfy the following conditions. If an even number ($2n$) of lines L_i are given in position, the ratio of the product of the first n of the d_i to the product of the remaining n d_i should be equal to the given ratio α/β, where α and β are arbitrary line segments. If an odd number ($2n - 1$) of lines L_i are given in position, the ratio of the product of the first n of the d_i to the product of the remaining $n-1$ d_i times a should be equal to the given ratio α/β. The case of three lines is exceptional, since it arises when two lines coincide in the four-line problem; the condition there is $(d_1 \cdot d_2)/(d_3)^2 = \alpha/\beta$. There are in fact points which satisfy each such condition, and they will form a locus on the plane.[23]

Apollonius, in investigating this problem, made use of a technique known as the application of areas, which reduces the given

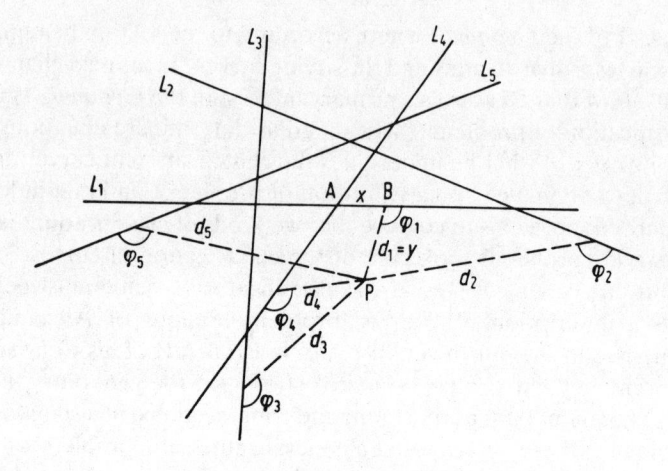

Fig. 1.4

problem to one of the geometrical transformation of areas. Thus, subordinate to his main goal of determining loci, he tried to express equivalences between areas (as in the case of four lines) in as short and simple a form as possible. Since the Greeks interpreted the products of two and three lines respectively as areas and volumes, the application of areas was ineffective beyond the case of six lines. Pappus, reporting on the work of Apollonius, hesitated to generalize beyond the case of six fixed lines, suggesting only that one might perhaps proceed by making use of continued proportions.[24]

In the middle of Book I Descartes describes his attack on the problem and then proudly announces, 'I believe that I have in this way completely accomplished what Pappus tells us the ancients sought to do',[25] as if he had solved the problem in a thoroughgoing way for any number of lines. While it is true that his combination of algebraic-arithmetical and geometrical results produces an important advance in the solution of the problem, it is not true that his treatment of the problem given in the *Geometry* is complete, according to his own methodological standards. Since Descartes believes that his starting-points are simple and easy to grasp and therefore unproblematic, and that his procedures for generating complexes out of them are transparent to reason, he must also believe that the advance of knowledge according to his method will be unobstructed and sure. Yet in fact there turn out to be unforeseen

Descartes's Geometry and Pappus' Problem

complexities in curves, in equations, and in the relations between them that call into question Descartes's claim and the confidence in his method on which it rests.

Descartes's explanation of how he proposes to solve this problem occurs at the end of Book I, accompanied by a diagram of its four-line version (Fig. 1.5). He chooses y equal to BC (d_1) and x equal to AB, and then shows how all the other d_i can be expressed linearly in x and y, by arguments which hinge on facts about similar triangles.[26] Then the proportions defining the conditions for the cases of 3, $2n$, and $2n-1$ lines given above can be rewritten as equations in x and y. For $2n$ lines, the equation will be of degree at most n; for $2n-1$ lines, it will be of degree at most n, but the highest power of x will be at most $n-1$. (For $2n$ and $2n-1$ parallel lines, where y is the sole variable involved, the result is an equation in y of degree at most n.)

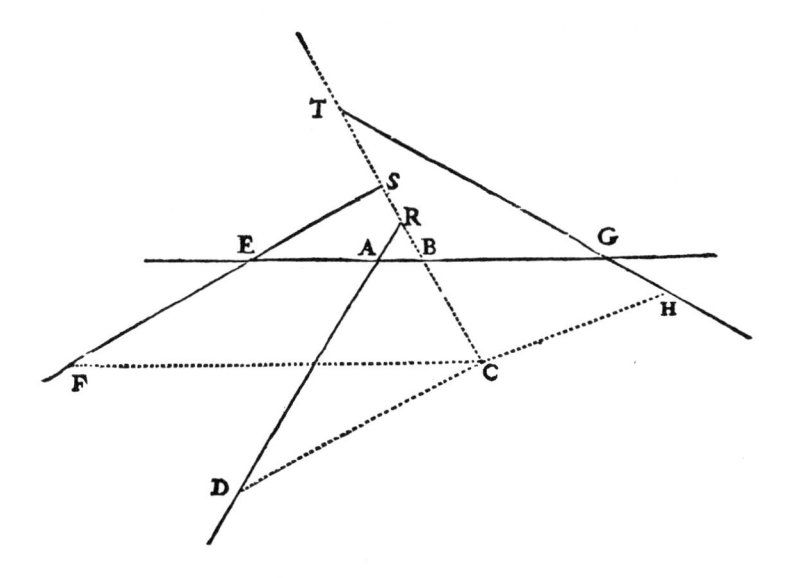

Fig. 1.5

The pointwise construction of the locus is then undertaken as follows. One chooses a value for y and plugs it into the equation, thus producing an equation in one unknown, x. For the case of three lines, the equation in x is in general of degree 2; for $2n$ lines, it is of degree at most n; and for $2n-1$ lines, it is of degree at most $n-1$.

(For $2n-1$ parallel lines, the equation already has only one variable, y, and is of degree n.) The roots of this equation can then be constructed by means of intersecting curves which must be decided upon; in the example of the quadratic equation from an earlier passage in Book I given above,[27] the choice is ruler and compass, that is, straight line and circle. This procedure generates the curve point by point and is thus potentially infinite, as Descartes notes: 'if then we should take successively an infinite number of values for the line y, we should obtain an infinite number of values for the line x, and therefore an infinity of different points, such as C, by means of which the required curve could be drawn'.[28] Thus it seems that Pappus' problem has been reduced to the geometrical construction of roots of equations in one unknown: the construction of line segments on the basis of rational relations among other line segments.

The combination of algebra and geometry is worthy of note. By rewriting the conditions of the problem as an equation, Descartes has converted it from a proportionality involving lines, areas, or volumes as terms (as it was in the classical formulation) to an equation about line segments. It has become an algebraic problem to which techniques for simplifying and solving equations can be applied. Yet it has not ceased to be a geometric problem as well, though the algebraic conversion has altered the geometry. The diagram is still centrally present, though it only involves straight line segments; no areas or volumes intervene here or as the focus of auxiliary constructions. The auxiliary constructions will be instead the construction of each x for a given y, using certain chosen curves as well as various geometrical theorems which must be antecedently available to the geometer. Because the problem can be viewed simultaneously as algebraic and geometrical, results from both fields can be brought to bear upon it, thus organizing and facilitating its solution. Also, Descartes's abstract statement of the procedure seems to impose no limits on the number of lines initially 'given in position', and thus to escape the stricture of the Greek formulation entirely.

Descartes's decision to give his treatment of Pappus' problem such a prominent position in the *Geometry* was quite wise, both rhetorically and rationally. Apropos the debate between ancients and moderns, Descartes's way of handling the problem is clearly superior and so nicely justifies his claim to rationalize geometry by

Descartes's Geometry and Pappus' Problem 33

means of his new method. And in so far as Descartes's new algebra-geometry will be one very important successor to classical geometry, no clearer justification of its rights as a successor could be made than its ability to solve a central and incompletely solved problem from the classical canon.

Yet Descartes's exploitation of Pappus' problem in the development of his new algebra-geometry is strikingly restricted. And his claims to have found a general solution are also not wholly justified; his abstract sketch of it is a promissory note which he was in no position to pay in full. I will argue that the former difficulty stems from the conceptual poverty of his official starting-points, and the latter from the rich diversity of what really constitutes the initiating ground of his project, a ground which his method leads him either to ignore or to bring in the back door, and in either case to leave uninspected.

The very first thing that Descartes says about his approach to Pappus' problem may seem odd if we expect him to be primarily interested in the loci which the problem generates.

First, I discovered that if the question be proposed for only three, four, or five lines, the required points can be found by elementary geometry, that is, by the use of the ruler and compasses only, and the application of those principles which I have already explained, except in the case of five parallel lines. In this case, and in the cases where there are six, seven, eight, or nine given lines, the required points can always be found by means of the geometry of solid loci, that is, by using some one of the three conic sections. Here, again, there is an exception in the case of nine parallel lines. For this and the cases of ten, eleven, twelve, or thirteen given lines, the required points may be found by means of a curve of level next higher [*degré plus composé*] than that of the conic sections. Again, the case of thirteen parallel lines must be excluded, for which, as well as for the cases of fourteen, fifteen, sixteen, and seventeen lines, a curve of level next higher [*degré plus composé*] than the preceding must be used; and so on indefinitely.[29]

For in this passage, he is classifying cases of the problem not by some feature of the locus generated, but rather by what kind of curve can be chosen in the pointwise construction of the locus, that is, in the construction of the line segment x given the relevant equation in x and y and a definite value of y. He iterates this classification of cases at the very end of Book I[30] in more explicitly algebraic terms. Otherwise stated, this classificatory scheme does not pertain to curves (describable by indeterminate equations in two unknowns) but to problems (describable by determinate equations in one unknown). Curves intervene in this passage only as constructing curves; each higher level of problem will require a constructing curve of higher level (*degré plus composé*).

Fig. 1.5 contains no hint of the locus, only the nexus of line segments with their specified relations to an arbitrary point C of the locus.[31] The implied auxiliary construction would be the determination of the line segment x by means of certain constructing curves, like Fig. 1.3 discussed earlier.[32] The official subject of these diagrams is line segments; constructing curves also intervene, but we have never been told *quid juris* and they are not what the diagram is about. Descartes's commitment to the methodological presupposition that his geometry is about line segments and their relations structures and narrows his whole enterprise.

Thus, Descartes's very first announcement concerning the Pappian cases is that he has discovered a way to generalize the classification of *problems*. And his reiteration of this classification is the ending of Book I. However, the announcement leaves vague what it means to say that the constructing curves which are required for each successive level of problems are of *degré plus composé*. Thus, Descartes's first way of grouping Pappian cases is supplemented by a second, which explicitly classifies loci. But I want to argue that the fact that this classification of loci is given second is quite significant. Descartes is not interested in classifying curves for their own sake; he undertakes this second classification in order to clarify the first, and regards the curves primarily as constructing curves. Here is the second grouping of Pappian cases.

> Next, I have found that when only three or four lines are given, the required points lie not only all on one of the conic sections but sometimes on the circumference of a circle or even on a straight line. When there are five, six, seven, or eight lines, the required points lie on a curve of level next higher [*degré plus composé*] than the conic sections, and it is impossible to imagine such a curve that may not satisfy the conditions of the problem; but the required points may possibly lie on a conic section, a circle, or a straight line. If there are nine, ten, eleven, or twelve lines, the required curve can be of level next higher [*degré plus composé*] than the preceding, but any such curve may meet the requirements, and so on to infinity.[33]

The vague notion of levels of complexity which Descartes invokes in this passage is later specified in terms of the 'genres' which he introduces in Book II to establish a hierarchy of curves, a ranking

Descartes's Geometry *and Pappus' Problem*

whose peculiarities I will examine in the next chapter. It is not clear from these remarks whether Descartes has any real acquaintance with curves beyond those already familiar from the classical canon, the circle and the conic sections. What do the new curves look like? What are their properties? Do they fall into discernible kinds? What new problems do they suggest? What new problems might they help solve? In the next chapter we will see that Descartes discovers a few new higher curves, but his discoveries are surprisingly restricted and he does not fully exploit the possibilities opened by his own new analytic geometry for investigating them.

Notes

1. *Discours de la Méthode*, HR i. 93; AT vi. 19–20.
2. Ibid., HR i. 92; AT vi. 19.
3. Euclid, *The Thirteen Books of Euclid's Elements*, ed. Sir Thomas Heath (3 vols.; New York: Dover, 1956), i. 153–5.
4. My comments here are informed by an unpublished paper by David Smigelskis (University of Chicago), entitled 'Namings, Showings and the Analytic Achievements of Appreciation'.
5. *La Géométrie* is one of the essays appended to the *Discours de la Méthode*, published in Leiden in 1637. In general I use the translation given in D. E. Smith and M. L. Latham (eds.), *The Geometry of Rene Descartes* (New York: Dover, 1954) though I emend it where noted. For each citation, I will give first the page numbers in Smith and Latham and then the page numbers from vol. vi. 367–485 of Adam and Tannery, where the *Geometry* is reprinted: in this case, 2–3; 369.
6. Ibid. 2–5; 369–70.
7. 'Meditations on Knowledge, Truth and Ideas', *Acta eruditorum*, Nov. 1684, reprinted in G. W. Leibniz, *Philosophical Papers and Letters*, ed. L. Loemker (Dordrecht: D. Reidel, 1956), 291–5.
8. *Dialogues Concerning Two New Sciences*, ed. H. Crew and A. de Salvo (New York: Dover, 1954), 173, 176.
9. See Galileo's letter to Paolo Sarpi, 1604 (*Le Opere di Galileo Galilei*, ed. A. Favaro (20 vols.; Florence: Edizione Nazionale, 1929–39), x. 115–16 and some associated documents discussed by E. Sylla in her 'Galileo and the Oxford Calculators', *Studies in Philosophy and the History of Philosophy*, 15, 53–108, esp. 68 f.
10. For an interesting discussion of this tradition, and its difference from the classical tradition, see E. Sylla's 'Compounding Ratios' in E. Mendelsohn (ed.) *Transformation and Tradition in the Sciences* (Cambridge: Cambridge University Press, 1984), 11–43. In this tradition, the terms of ratios are taken to be numbers only, and ratios are identified with their 'sizes' or 'denominationes', i.e. the number expressing the ratio in lowest terms. This tradition tends to restrict the concept of number to the rational numbers. The extension of the number concept one might expect from the identification of a line segment with 'number', i.e. what algebra is about, is thus counteracted.
11. *La Géométrie*, pp. 4–5; 370.
12. Sylla notes that these assumptions belong to the medieval, not the classical, tradition of handling proportions, in her 'Compounding Ratios'. I discuss this point again in Ch. 2.

Descartes's Geometry and Pappus' Problem 37

13. Euclid, *Elements*, bk. VI in ii. 187–221.
14. *La Géométrie*, pp. 4–5; 370–1.
15. Ibid. 12–15; 374–5.
16. Euclid, *Elements*, bk. I, prop. 47 in i. 349–50.
17. C. B. Boyer, *A History of Mathematics* (Princeton: Princeton University Press, 1985), 75–6.
18. Ibid. 140–2.
19. *La Géométrie*, pp. 78–81; 406–7.
20. Ibid. 92–5, 412–13. Pp. 92–113, 412–23, expound the double-root method for determining normals to curves, but H. J. M. Bos notes that it is a side-issue within the book as a whole in his 'The Structure of Descartes' *Géométrie*', *Atti del Covegno Internazionale 'Descartes: il Discorso sul Metodo e i Saggi di questo Metodo'*, Lecce, 22–4 Oct. 1987.
21. P. Fermat, *Œuvres*, ed. P. Tannery and C. Henry (4 vols.; Paris: Gauthier-Villars, 1891–1912), i. 92–103.
22. Boyer, *History of Mathematics*, p. 209.
23. Bos gives a lucid description of Pappus' problem in his 'On the Representation of Curves in Descartes' *Géométrie*', *Archive for History of the Exact Sciences*, 24 (1981), 295–338, esp. 298–302. For another interesting discussion of this problem in relation to its classical antecedents, see A. G. Molland, 'Shifting the Foundations: Descartes' Transformation of Ancient Geometry', *Historia Mathematica*, 3 (1976) 21–49.
24. Boyer, *History of Analytic Geometry* (New York: Scripta Mathematica, 1956), 37–9.
25. *La Géométrie*, pp. 26–7, 382.
26. Ibid. 26–9, 382–3.
27. Ibid. 12–15, 374–5.
28. Ibid. 34–5, 386.
29. Ibid. 23–5, 380–1. In this passage, Smith and Latham translate '*degré plus composé*' as 'next highest degree'. This must be incorrect. Descartes uses the word 'dimension' for our algebraic notion of the degree of the equation associated with a curve. What Descartes means by '*degré*' here is vague, but he makes it precise later on in terms of the notion of 'genre'. Thus I have translated the word here by the somewhat vague locution 'level'.
30. Ibid. 34–7, 386–7.
31. Ibid. 26–7, 382. Descartes does include the locus, as a circle, hyperbola, and Cartesian parabola, in related diagrams in bk II.
32. Ibid. 12–15, 374–5.
33. Ibid. 24–7, 381.

2
Treatment of Curves: Notion of Genre

THE title of Book II of the *Geometry* is 'On·the Nature of Curved Lines', but the very first thing Descartes says to introduce the chapter refers to the classification of problems, and underlines the fact that he is thinking of curves first and foremost as constructing curves.

The ancients were familiar with the fact that the problems of geometry may be divided into three classes, namely, plane, solid, and linear problems. This is equivalent to saying that some problems require a conic section and still others require more complex [*plus composé*] curves. I am surprised, however, that they did not go further, and distinguish between different levels [*degrés*] of these more complex [*plus composé*] curves, nor do I see why they called the latter mechanical, rather than geometrical.[1]

Descartes sees the central task which he inherits from the Greeks as the classification of problems by means of the constructing curves needed to find each solution. His rationalization of the field consists primarily in clarifying the level of problems occurring after those called solid. According to Descartes's critical limitation of the domain of geometry, transcendental curves are never appropriate means of construction for such problems; instead, he proposes higher algebraic curves, and in particular a certain cubic which has come to be known as the Cartesian parabola. Significantly, Descartes does not say that the ancients missed out on many important curves because they were not able to use the algebraic equation as a way of expressing and analysing curves. For Descartes, algebra is not an originating source from which items, problems, and solutions might arise, but only a device for information-storage, bookkeeping, and abbreviation.[2] Rather, he points to their failure to generalize their means of construction and to submit those means to rational constraints.

Historically, Descartes's earliest interest in geometry centred on how geometrical problems could be constructed by tracing-machines which are generalizations of ruler and compass, two of

Treatment of Curves: Notion of Genre 39

which he discusses in the opening pages of Book II.[3] What is the relation of this discussion to the matter of Book I, and how does it fit into the 'order of reasons'? We saw in Book I that the availability (i.e. construction) of straight line segments representing products, quotients, and square roots requires the prior availability of curves (circles) and of theorems about triangles. Descartes's claim that the starting-points of his *Geometry* are straight line segments covers over his exclusion of areas and curves, *inter alia*, and his unacknowledged reliance upon them. Another way the same point can be made in the context of Book II is that Descartes has already assumed in Book I the availability of tracing-machines along with the mathematical items and assumptions they embody, without explicitly giving them a place in the order of reasons, since in fact they would disrupt the order he claims to be establishing.

But here at the beginning of Book II he brings them in explicitly, as part of his programme of rationalizing classical geometry. Descartes is forced to appeal to his tracing-machines as a source of constructing curves and as a way to fix and maintain a hierarchy of such curves. Book I does not reliably provide this source and guarantee, for the following reasons. The pointwise construction of curves articulated in Descartes's solution to Pappus' problem looks like a way to generate more and more complex loci, higher algebraic curves, starting from rational relations among line segments (if we close our eyes to the various assumptions Descartes smuggles into that solution). But as we noted, Descartes views these loci primarily as potential constructing curves. The indefinitely iterated, pointwise construction of curves will not guarantee the existence of all the points of intersection required when curves are used as means of construction.[4] Moreover, Descartes does not regard the algebraic equation alone as a respectable way to generate curves. The order of reasons so far has not provided existence conditions strong enough to provide constructing curves.

Not only that, but the pointwise construction of curves as the only way of generating curves, despite its apparent fidelity to the order of reasons, threatens the stability of the hierarchy of problems (and the hierarchy of curves subordinate to it) which Descartes is trying to establish. Descartes wants to establish the levels of his hierarchy by showing, for example, that problems of a certain kind cannot be constructed by conic sections but require a curve of higher genre. However, if this curve of higher genre can itself be constructed pointwise by conic sections and if conic sections can be constructed pointwise by ruler and compass, then in a strong sense, the whole problem can be constructed by ruler and compass. All that is needed for any construction is ruler and compass, and the articulation of the hierarchy collapses back to its lowest level.[5]

My point here is not a mere logical nicety, but indicates a serious difficulty with the reductionism of Cartesian method. On the one hand it requires purity and homogeneity in its subject-matter; everything which belongs to a domain must originate in the given starting-points, and nothing alien can be admitted. On the other hand, the order of reasons presents itself as an articulated, stratified order, with levels that occur one after the other. The difficulty which Descartes encounters at the beginning of Book II exhibits the tension between the demand for homogeneity and the demand for articulation inherent in his method. To get his hierarchy to stand, Descartes must violate the allegedly homogeneous unfolding of his order of reasons, and he does so by inserting his tracing-machines into the argument at this point.

DESCARTES'S NOTION OF GENRE

In the opening paragraph of Book II just quoted, Descartes announces that he is going to correct and replace the Greek classification of problems into plane, solid, and linear by a new one rationalized by the proper use of method. The Greek classification arises from distinctions among the means of construction used to solve problems; plane problems are solvable by straight line and circle (ruler and compass), solid problems by conic section, and linear problems, a grab-bag category, by all other means, including some transcendental curves. Descartes perceives the error of this classification as stemming from confusion about the nature of curves, which, as I have so often stressed, he thinks of primarily as constructing curves. He will clear up this confusion by establishing a hierarchy of 'genres' of curves, to undergird a hierarchy of 'genres' of problems, And with the enthusiastic summation of this latter hierarchy, he ends the *Geometry*, as if this were his most important contribution to mathematics.[6]

Descartes's definition of 'genre' apropos curves occurs in the midst of his discussion of two tracing machines in the first pages of Book II. He explains why they are acceptable generalizations of

Treatment of Curves: Notion of Genre

ruler and compass, and therefore likely sources where constructing curves for supersolid problems might show up. (Later on in Book II he discusses tracing procedures which generate transcendental curves, and explains that they are unacceptable generalizations of ruler and compass because the comparison of the motions involved requires forming ratios between straight and curved line segments.)[7]

Descartes's first tracing-machine (Fig. 2.1) is a system of linked rulers which allows the user to find one, two, three, or more mean proportionals between two given line segments.[8] This is, clearly, an ordered series of problems. Notice that the implied constructions depend, among other things, on properties of the circle and of similar triangles. As it is opened, the machine traces out certain curves AD, AF, AH, and so on, which then function as constructing curves, since their intersections with the circles determine the sought-for line segments, the mean proportionals. Descartes recognizes that these constructing curves form a series of higher algebraic curves of increasing complexity, though he does not give an equation for any of them.[9]

Descartes presents this machine as an embodiment or manifestation of the order of reasons, which generates increasingly complex items out of the clear and distinct simples of geometry, straight line segments and their proportions. Once again, Descartes does not

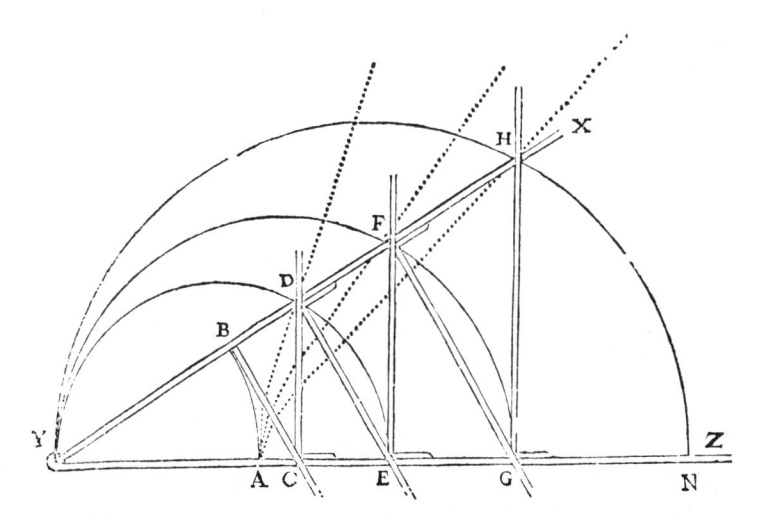

Fig. 2.1

examine what might disrupt that order, the mathematical truths about circles and similar triangles which the very employment of the hinged rulers depends upon. He has also raised a difficulty: what is the relation of this order of reasons, this particular series of problems and constructing curves generated by the hinged rulers, to the order established in Book I, the two series (problems and curves) of the Pappian cases?

As I suggested earlier, I believe that for both historical and logical reasons, Descartes cannot wholly integrate the two progressions of Book I and Book II. But he tries to assimilate the two distinct series of curves under the general claim that 'the best way to group together all such curves and then classify them in order, is by recognizing the fact that all points of those curves which we may call "geometric", that is, those that fall under some precise and exact measure, necessarily have a relation to all the points of a straight line, which can be expressed by some equation, the same for all.'[10] However, if this criterion encompassed both series of curves equally and adequately, Descartes could stop with the Pappian cases and would not have to introduce the fresh start of tracing-machines, disrupting the order of reasons. But the pointwise construction of curves as Pappian loci does not provide the strong continuity required for constructing curves. That Descartes must augment pointwise construction with mechanical tracing testifies to a well-founded worry that the two series do not come to the same thing.

Another, related difficulty arises here. Descartes's pointwise construction of curves as Pappian loci presupposes not only rational relations among line segments, but also the prior availability of constructing curves, as my exposition of Book I is at pains to point out. It would be reasonable to require Descartes to provide tracings by continuous motion for these constructing curves at least, if not for the whole complement of Pappian loci. While Descartes is careful to provide such tracings, even and especially for the Cartesian parabola, he has no way of proving he can provide them in general, for all the requisite (and yet to be discovered) constructing curves.[11]

Descartes simply cannot rely on his tracing-machines alone to generate complete series of problems and curves. The series they generate are too special. His hinged rulers, for example, do not produce the curve he is most interested in exhibiting as the fruit of his method, the Cartesian parabola. And a little further on in Book

II he gives a pointwise construction of a Pappian locus for which he cannot furnish any kind of tracing by continuous motion.[12] By contrast, Descartes believes that every algebraic curve can be generated as a Pappian locus. (This belief is false.)[13] So the Pappian series (apparently) gives him all the curves he wants, but not strongly enough, and the hinged rulers give him curves with stronger existence conditions, but not enough of them.

At this point in his argument, Descartes presents his definition of 'genre', intended to clarify the vague locution '*degré plus composé*', in terms of the equation associated with the curve.

If this equation contains no term of higher degree than the rectangle of two unknown quantities, or the square of one [Et que lorsque cette equation ne monte que jusque au rectangle de deux quantités indéterminées, ou bien au quarré d'une même] the curve belongs to the first and simplest genre, which contains only the circle, the parabola, the hyperbola, and the ellipse; but when the equation contains one or more terms of the third or fourth degree in one or both of the two unknown quantities [mais que lorsque l'equation monte jusque à la trois ou quatrième dimension des deux, ou de l'une des deux quantités indéterminées] . . . the curve belongs to the second genre; and if the equation contains a term of the fifth and sixth degree in either or both of the unknown quantities [et que lorsque l'equation monte jusque à la cinquième ou sixième dimension] the curve belongs to the third genre, and so on indefinitely.[14]

Though this classification of curves refers to the equation, it is not simply algebraic, for then Descartes would have no need to appeal to anything besides the degree of the equation, as a classificatory mark and a measure of complexity which can thus order curves. Instead, he puts curves of first and second degree, lines, circles, and the conic sections, together in one genre; curves of third and fourth degree go together in the second genre; curves of fifth and sixth degree in the third genre, and so forth. Why does he do this?

There are at least three reasons why Descartes sets up his classification this way, and each indicates that Descartes was thinking of curves not as objects of interest in their own right, but as means of construction in the solution of problems. Each reason also involves an unfounded generalization, a rash extrapolation, which again unmasks Descartes's faith in the ability of his method to lead from simple and easy starting-points to cases of greater and greater complexity with a kind of transparent, unproblematic reasonableness. He sums up this particular article of his methodology in the penultimate line of the *Geometry*: 'It is only necessary to follow the same general method to construct all problems, more and more complex, ad infinitum; for in the case of mathematical progressions, whenever the first two or three terms are given, it easy to find the rest.'[15] Descartes assumes that there are no hidden depths in the starting-points, the network of rational relations raised upon them, nor the interaction between those two dimensions of the discovery process. All these reductionist assumptions turn out to be wrong.

The first reason which Descartes gives for construing genres as pairs of degrees has to do with the second tracing-machine, presented immediately after his definition of genre (Fig. 2.2). This machine generates new, more complex curves from the motion of simpler curves and straight lines. GL is linked to the device NKL at L; as L slides up or down the vertical axis, GL turns around G. The intersections of the line KNC and GL trace out a curve; in this case Descartes identifies it as a hyperbola and writes an equation for it: $y^2 = cy - c/b\, xy + ay - ac$.[16] Thus, when a straight line is put into the machine, it generates a curve of the first genre. When a circle is put into the machine, the intersections of KNC and GL trace

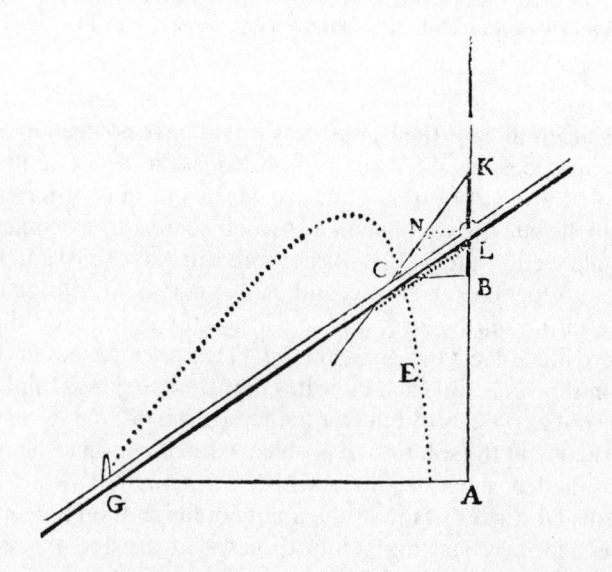

Fig. 2.2

out a conchoid, which is of a higher genre than the circle. And when the curve KNC is a parabola, its intersections with GL trace out the 'Cartesian parabola', which is also of a higher genre than the parabola.

The upshot of all this is that Descartes believes that this particular tracing-machine will yield, when a given curve is plugged into it, a more complex curve of the next highest genre. He claims, for example, that if a curve of the second genre were used in the tracing, a curve of the third genre would be produced, and so forth, *ad infinitum*.[17] Thus, this machine seems to provide the rigid, non-collapsible stratification that Descartes's method requires of a hierarchy. Curves of different genres are held separate by the required mediating action of the machine.

Like the hinged rulers, this second machine is not alleged to produce the complete set of plane algebraic curves, but it does produce the Cartesian parabola, whose importance I will discuss shortly. Descartes's motley collection of tracing-machines (he mentions that he could give other examples of them) generates only small families of curves, as it were, not the whole population, but does so with the stronger guarantee of continuity which constructing curves require. Descartes appeals to the tracing-machine because he needs that guarantee; and because the machine appears to stratify curves by pairs of algebraic degree, he builds that feature into his definition of genre.

But he generalizes without proof, and his generalization is wrong. (In a sense Cartesian method is designed to obviate the need for proof.)[18] The curve whose equation is $y^3 = c^2z$ provides a counter-example; when it serves as the moving curve, its intersections with the line GL trace out a curve of fourth degree, which is of the same genre.[19] Moreover, Descartes's inability to claim any sort of completeness for the set of curves this tracing-machine generates is grave. The fact that it furnishes the Cartesian parabola, which becomes the canonical constructing curve for the next, supersolid level of problems, is no guarantee that it (or any other tracing-machine) will generate the required constructing curves for all the higher levels.

Right after his description of the second tracing-machine, Descartes reiterates his classification of curves by genre, and gives a second reason for associating pairs of degrees in each genre. 'This classification is based upon the fact that there is a general rule for reducing to a cubic any problem of the fourth degree, and to a problem of the fifth degree any problem of the sixth degree, so that the latter in each case need not be considered any more complex than the former. [Il y a reigle generale pour reduire au cube toutes les difficultés qui vont au quarré de quarré, et au sursolide toutes celles qui vont au quarré de cube, de façon qu'on ne les doit point estimer plus composé.]'[20] Here Descartes probably had in mind Ferrari's rule for reducing equations of fourth degree in one unknown to ones of third degree.[21] But there is no such rule for equations of sixth and fifth degree, and so the extrapolation is unfounded. Moreover, Ferrari's rule is about equations in one unknown, which correspond to problems, not to curves; indeed, Descartes speaks here not of *lignes courbes* but of *difficultés*. He is thus justifying his way of classifying curves by an appeal to the reduction of one kind of problem to another. This is a very strange move and, I think, an indication of the extent to which for Descartes the study of curves is subordinate to the study of problems, i.e. rational relations among straight line segments. Thus the classification of curves is an unstable project for Descartes which as such cannot quite come into focus, and it immediately transforms into a classification of problems.

The third and deepest reason for Descartes's way of classifying curves by genre reveals the significance of the second reason for him. It does not become explicit until Book III, entitled 'On the Construction of Solid or Supersolid Problems'. Descartes has shown in Book I that problems whose associated equation in one unknown is of degree at most 2 can be solved by ruler and compass. Descartes begins Book III by discussing a variety of problems, the equations associated with them, and the constructing curves needed to solve them, and summarizes his results with a 'general rule'. Make sure your equation (in one unknown) is reduced to its simplest form, he says, and then if it is of third or fourth degree, the problem is solid and the required constructing curves will be conic sections: indeed, one need employ only a circle and a parabola to solve all such problems.[22] And if the equation is of fifth or sixth degree, the problem belongs to the level next beyond solid. He goes on to solve a variety of solid problems by circle and parabola constructions, and then remarks that more complex problems require constructing curves which are themselves more complex than the conics.[23] At this point he reintroduces the Cartesian parabola, to

Treatment of Curves: Notion of Genre 47

serve, along with the circle, as the pertinent constructing curve for problems at the next, supersolid level.

The Cartesian parabola is one of the very few cubics with which Descartes is really familiar. He derives it in Book II as the locus in a special case of the five-line Pappus' problem, where there are four equidistant parallel lines and a fifth line perpendicular to the others 'given in position', and where the relevant ϕ_i are right angles (Fig. 2.3) In this diagram, he combines the nexus of lines for the Pappian case just described with, superimposed upon it, the second tracing-machine, where a parabola has been plugged in. Thus, in this diagram the series of Pappian cases and the series generated by his second tracing-machine converge. Descartes can furnish both a pointwise construction of the curve, and trace it continuously by

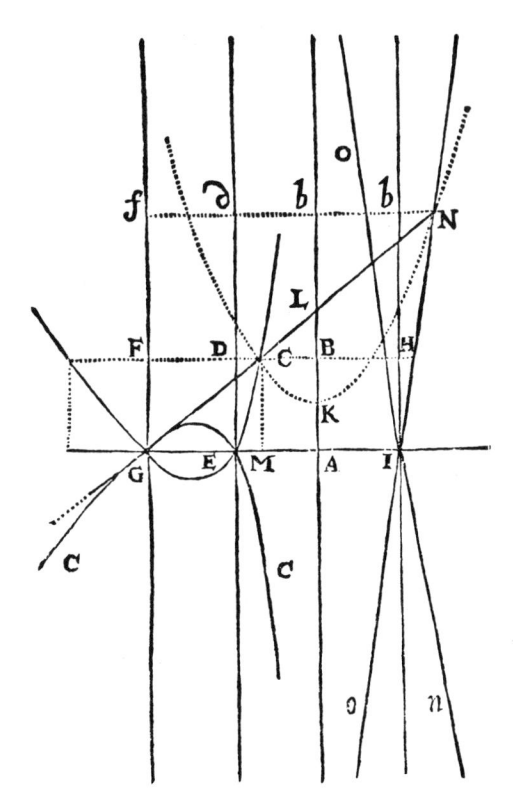

Fig. 2.3

one of his machines. And, as he shows, both the pointwise construction and the tracing yield the same equation, $y^3 - 2ay^2 - a^2y + 2a^3 = axy$.[24] The Cartesian parabola is then a respectable constructing curve, and is just what Descartes requires for the next, supersolid level of problems. He demonstrates this in the final pages of Book III, where he uses it as the constructing curve to solve the class of problems associated with the sixth-degree equation of general form, $y^6 - py^5 + qy^4 - ry^3 + sy^2 - ty + u = 0$.[25]

Descartes then restates his 'general rule' on the last page of Book III, and of course of the *Geometry* as a whole. Significantly, in this passage he uses the word 'genre' to refer not to curves, but to problems, claiming that he has just reduced to a single construction all problems of the same genre: 'reduit à une même construction tous les Problèmes d'un même genre'.

> Having constructed all plane problems by the cutting of a circle by a straight line, and all solid problems by the cutting of a circle by a parabola, and, finally, all that are but one level more complex [d'un degré plus composé] by cutting a circle by a curve only one level higher [d'un degré plus composé] than the parabola, it is only necessary to follow the same general method to construct all problems, more and more complex ad infinitum [qui sont plus composés à l'infini]; for in the case of mathematical progressions, whenever the first two or three terms are given, it is easy to find the rest.[26]

The introduction of one higher curve as a means of construction apparently allows the construction of roots of equations in one unknown of two successive higher degrees. The introduction of the parabola covers problems whose associated equations are of degrees 3 and 4, and the Cartesian parabola covers equations of degrees 5 and 6. This strongly suggests to Descartes that equations (in one unknown) of degrees $2n-1$ and $2n$ go together, and in this final passage he groups problems in this way, using the word 'genre'. Thus too he suggests that problems of genre n (where $n>1$) should be solvable by some canonical curve of genre $n-1$.[27]

Descartes's reason for classifying curves into genres in Book II is primarily to provide constructing curves for higher genres of problems. His reasons for associating equations of degree $2n-1$ and $2n$ pertain not to the equations in two unknowns which correspond to curves, but to equations in one unknown which correspond to problems. And yet his habit of transposing inquiry into curves back to inquiry into problems, of decomposing curves into indefinitely

Treatment of Curves: Notion of Genre

iterated cases of rational relations among straight line segments, leads him to associate curve-equations of degrees $2n-1$ and $2n$ as well. This is my explanation of Descartes's peculiar notion of genre.

On the basis of this, I can also explain why Descartes knows so little about cubic (and quartic and higher) curves, and why this does not bother him, despite his own method's demand for completeness in expositions of this kind. My general claim is that Descartes is not interested in the investigation of higher curves as such, but rather in 'higher problems' and the constructing curves needed to solve them. Since one new constructing curve of a given genre n, like the Cartesian parabola, suffices for the solution of a whole class of problems of genre $n + 1$, there is simply no need to catalogue the higher genres of curves and discover all their sub-kinds. (Newton is the first to almost master the cubics; he catalogues seventy-two sub-kinds and even so omits six.) For Descartes, one good constructing curve as the representative of each higher genre will be sufficient.

Descartes does investigate one group of curves of the second genre, his optical ovals. But his treatment of them is characteristically off-centre. He introduces one of them as an illustration of his method of constructing normals, with a diagram (Fig. 2.4) where the centre of interest is not the curve but the problem, the construction of the line segment CP, the normal to the curve at the point C.[28] When he discusses them in order to exhibit their optical properties, he generates them by pointwise construction.[29] Nowhere does he give an equation for one of them, though he does use algebra to discuss their properties. Optics presents Descartes with a series of problems concerning the conditions under which reflected light rays (straight line segments) will converge at a given point. It is the construction of the point of convergence which interests Descartes, not the curve of the curved reflecting surface. He prefaces and

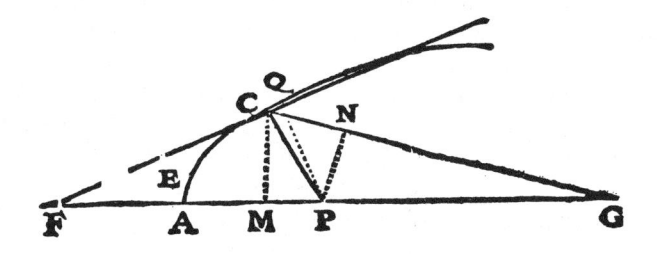

Fig. 2.4

closes his treatment of the optical ovals with an assertion of their usefulness to optics, as if one would not be interested in the study of curves for their own sake. In the end, the only higher curve which Descartes understands in the thoroughgoing, multivalent fashion that characterizes the important investigations of curves at the end of the century is the Cartesian parabola.

CARTESIAN PROPORTIONS

My quarrel with Descartes is not that I think pointwise construction and mechanical tracing are somehow defective ways to introduce curves. In mathematical invention, one needs to exploit whatever stratagems are available. I do think that trying to reduce curves to points and lines, or to ideal instruments that can construct them is philosophically misguided, since inquiry into what makes a curve a curve, which is the propaedeutic for generating interesting problems about curves, must first pay attention to its peculiar integrity. Nor do I think that Descartes ought to have introduced curves by the algebraic equation alone, as if that would have solved his mathematical quandaries.

My quarrel with Descartes is rather that he tries to shut out a whole range of interesting possibilities for geometry and its offspring, among them certain investigations of curves. One of my central reproaches in this regard is his insistence on a kind of homogeneity in the terms of proportions. And a second is that he misses the import of his abstract relational structure, and how it allows the combination of knowledge about numbers, ways of articulating space, and equations so that, among other things, curves can be regarded as hybrids. Both these narrowings of vision result from his reductionist conception of method, which never achieves adequate purchase on the unity of complex wholes. At this point I will turn my attention from what Descartes actually did in the *Geometry* and how his method shaped it, to what he might have done if his method had not diverted him from it. My aim here is not so much anachronistically to demand of Descartes that he produce the work of his inheritors, but rather to make some fundamental observations about the nature of geometry, and its relation to other mathematical domains and to physics as well.

Euclid views a ratio as 'a kind of relation in respect of size between two magnitudes of the same kind', and a proportion as an

Treatment of Curves: Notion of Genre 51

assertion of similitude between two such relations. This view is expounded in Book V of the *Elements*, and it is applicable to magnitudes of every kind.[30] In Book VI the general theory of ratio is applied to ratios between geometrical magnitudes, irrational as well as rational, and in Book VII and succeeding books to ratios between numbers (integers). The leading principle of this theory of ratio is the Eudoxian or Archimedean axiom, which states: 'Magnitudes are said to have a ratio to one another which are capable, when multiplied, of exceeding one another.'[31] In other words, one can form a ratio A : B (where A < B) if and only if there is a positive integer n such that $nA > B$.

This principle illustrates a salient feature of classical mathematics noted earlier, which is that the mathematical entities which might possibly serve as terms are treated as heterogeneous kinds, each with its own peculiar integrity: numbers, line segments, shaped surfaces, shaped volumes, curves, rational and irrational magnitudes, finite and infinitesimal magnitudes. This integrity must be accounted for (as in the Definitions, Postulates and Common Notions of Book I of the *Elements*)[32] and respected. Specifically, when terms are associated in the formation of ratios and proportions, their association must be carefully justified, and may sometimes be proscribed.

Thus, the Eudoxian axiom allows the conjunction of two integers, or two line segments, or two areas in a ratio, but proscribes that of a number and a geometrical magnitude, of two geometrical magnitudes of different dimensions, and of a finite and infinitesimal, or a finite and infinite, magnitude. Aristotle is concerned with the same issue when he proscribes ratios between curved and straight lines, and in his analysis of the continuum, between finite and infinitesimal or finite and infinite, magnitudes.[33] Of course, this enforcing of a certain homogeneity between terms in a ratio entails a segregation of mathematical entities and prevents various strategies of unification and generalization which we have seen in incipient form in Descartes's *Geometry*.

However, the Eudoxian axiom also tolerates an important kind of heterogeneity between two terms yoked in a ratio: one may be an irrational magnitude when the other is a rational magnitude. For example, it allows the expression and manipulation of ratios between a side S and the hypotenuse H of a right isosceles triangle whose equal sides are one unit. This axiom is justly famous for legitimizing the introduction of irrational magnitudes into classical mathematics. In effect, it allows ' : ' to be treated as a virtual, not actually completed operation which can link S and H even though the operation S : H cannot be carried out as it can in the case of 4 : 2. Thus, the nature of the association of S and H in the ratio S : H not only treats S and H as mutually heterogeneous but also treats the ratio S : H as a third kind of thing, different from either S or H.

The Euclidean tradition in general treats ratios as relations, different from the terms related. And it acknowledges the heterogeneity of terms on the one hand by carefully segregating them and on the other hand by allowing their association under certain conditions. Moreover, it monitors the association of ratios in proportions. For this tradition, proportions are not claims about equality but rather similitude. The assertion of a likeness between a ratio holding between terms of one kind, and a ratio holding between terms of another kind, is not automatic but must be carefully regulated and justified. It is as if ratios too are infected by the heterogeneity of their component terms.

The condition for asserting $A : B :: C : D$ could not be that $A \times D = B \times C$, for A and B might be of a different kind from C and D, and hence the products of A and D, or B and C might not be interpretable, especially since geometric quantities lack a multiplicative structure. Rather, Euclid gives the condition in Book V, Definition 5 of the *Elements* by generalizing the Eudoxian axiom: A proportion between continuous or non-continuous ratios $A : B$ and $C : D$ can be formed if and only if for all positive integers m and n, when $nA \lesseqgtr mB$, then correspondingly $nC \lesseqgtr mD$.[34] (If the two ratios happened to be continuous, so that the second term of the first were the first term of the second, the homogeneity of all the terms would be guaranteed by the condition for forming ratios.)

Descartes's method requires homogeneity in the starting-points of geometry and thus in the terms which can figure in proportions: they must all be straight line segments. He never admits that this was a choice among alternatives, and that his choice involves conflations, analogies, and exclusions. In fact, his choice aligns him with a second tradition of handling proportions, distinct from the Euclidean, that impoverishes mathematics even as it opens up new possibilities. Descartes never explicitly discusses the theory of proportions which allows him to associate simples; to do so would have disrupted the order of reasons.

The second, medieval tradition of handling ratios and proportions contrasts strongly with the Euclidean. It appears to originate with Theon, a commentator on Ptolemy's *Almagest*, and is transmitted in the Middle Ages by Jordanus Nemorarius, Campanus, and Roger Bacon. It associates with each ratio a 'denomination', that is, a number which gives its 'size', and in general treats the magnitudes occurring in ratios uniformly as numbers. Thus ratios are just quotients, and the distinction between terms and ratios is abolished, in so far as they are all numbers. The condition $A \times D = B \times C$ now self-evidently guarantees that the proportion $A:B::C:D$, or more accurately $A/B = C/D$, holds. Proportions are no longer assertions of similitude between ratios, but of equality between numbers. Significantly, this treatment of proportion in the late Middle Ages tended to restrict the then unstable concept of number to the rationals by requiring that division be an operation which could be carried out in familiar ways.[35]

Descartes's treatment of ratios and proportions clearly belongs to this second tradition. In his exposition of multiplication on the second page of the *Geometry*, for example, he infers from the proportion $BA:BD::BC:BE$ that $BE \times BA = BD \times BC$ without further comment; there is no need to worry about the association of terms in a non-continuous proportion, since the terms and their ratios (quotients) and products are all homogeneous in a strong sense.[36] Of course, Descartes chooses line segments, not numbers, to be his homogeneous set of terms.

What follows from Descartes's insistence on the homogeneity of terms? Primarily, it limits his mathematics. Among the most mathematically inventive of Descartes's contemporaries (Cavalieri, Galileo, and Torricelli in Italy, Wallis in England), experimentation with the possibilities of ratios and proportions involving lines and areas, straight and curved lines, and finite and infinitesimal magnitudes (of various dimensions) are already at the forefront of mathematical researches that will lead to the calculus. And such reasonings in the work of Leibniz and Newton prove to be keys to the application of mathematics to dynamical problems.[37]

An example of the way in which Descartes's methodological presuppositions hamper his ability to open the frontiers of mathematical research is his solution to 'Debeaune's Problem'. In 1638, shortly after the publication of the *Geometry*, Debeaune posed Descartes the following problem: 'What curve has the property, that its ordinate y bears the same relation to its subtangent t as the difference of its abscissa x and ordinate y to a given magnitude a?'[38]

Descartes gives two solutions to the problem. The first is a pointwise construction of the curve using approximative methods, illustrated in Fig. 2.5. Descartes proceeds by zeroing in on each point of the curve AVX, as the limit of the intersection of two neighbouring tangents GDX and VDN by means of a complicated nexus of auxiliary constructions. He divides the line segment AB = b into m equal pieces, and stipulates that PV = nb/m and RX = $(n-1)b/m$ ($0 < n < m$). The line segment FD occurs in two proportions, FD : FN = PV : PN and FD : FM = RX : RM, which yields, via a set of equations and the assumption that PN = RM, the difference of the y coordinates of the points X and V as bounded by two values, $b/n < \beta - \alpha < b/(n-1)$. This procedure works for any two pairs of points on the curve; applied to A and V, and with $m=8$, $n=6$, it gives $(1/8+1/7)b < \alpha < (1/7+1/6)b$. The more parts AB=$b$ is divided into, the finer an approximation. In general, the x coordinate of the point sought will be its distance from the curve's asymptote RCM, expressed as some fraction n/m of b, and the y coordinate can be approximated as

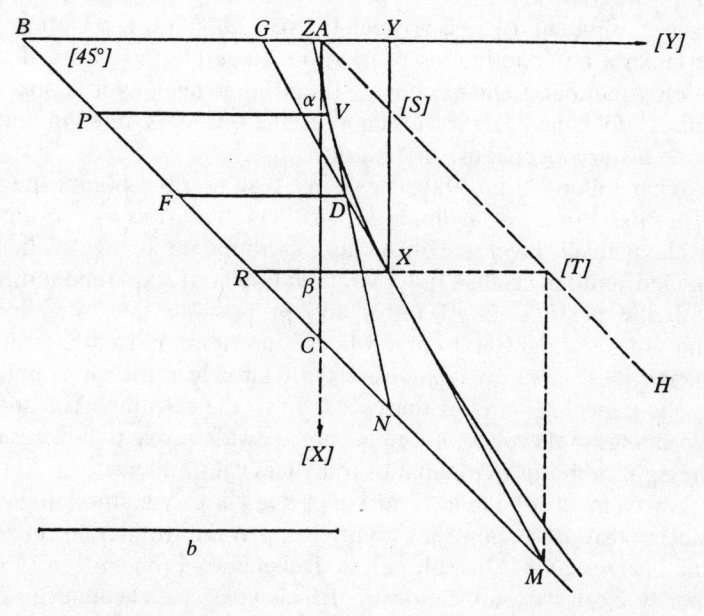

Fig. 2.5

Treatment of Curves: Notion of Genre

$$(1/m+1/(m-1) + \ldots + 1/(n+1))b < y < (1/(m-1)+1/(m-2) + \ldots +1/n)b.^{39}$$

The proof is to my mind fussy; there is no obvious way to generalize the construction of the curve and no suggestion of a family of curves to which it might belong. Descartes's pointwise handling of the problem through auxiliary constructions involving subdivided line segments obscures the character of the curve as a whole and interferes with his ability to see the intrinsic interest of the problem. And the situation is no better with Descartes's second solution, which traces the curve through the intersection of two moving lines. Let the line AH move parallel to itself and to the left at a constant velocity v; and let the line BA move downward, parallel to itself, starting at the same moment with velocity v, but increasing in velocity in the following way: it reaches $(8/7)v$ when the first line has gone a distance $b/8$, $(8/6)v$ when the first line has gone $2b/8$, and so forth.[40] Descartes regards these two movements as incommensurable, and concludes that this mechanical curve does not belong to geometry. He nowhere mentions that it is logarithmic, which is ultimately the reason why it is interesting. And indeed, Descartes had found the logarithmic relation worthy of study in other contexts, the compounding of interest and the *linea proportionum*.[41]

It is noteworthy that Descartes's solution to Debeaune's problem involves infinitary procedures at two stages: the approximation of the coordinate y given an x, and the pointwise construction of the curve. Descartes is often called a finitist, but the nature of his finitism bears some clarification. I suggest that as long as the line segments figuring as terms in the proportions are finite, Descartes has nothing against certain kinds of infinite iteration. Indeed, they are his way of moving from simples to complexes without giving up the homogeneity his method requires. But the linking of a finite line segment and, for example, an infinitesimal line segment in a proportion would have been anathema to him, the very archetype of irrationality. This seems ironic when we recall that Leibniz's solution to Debeaune's problem, a curve-equation which he finds fascinating precisely because it is a transcendental curve, hinges on giving its defining condition in the form of a proportion between the ratios dy/dx and $(x-y)/a$.[42]

Descartes's commitment to the homogeneity of terms which his method imposes generates further difficulties for him. The differences between certain kinds of mathematical entities may sometimes be as important as their similarities. Another way of saying this is, when different kinds of mathematical entities are assimilated to each other, it may be important to remember that the assimilation is only one of analogy, not identity. For analogies need justification, have limits, and tend to grow beyond themselves. When Descartes takes line segments as terms but uses a theory of proportions designed for rational numbers, he is in effect setting up an analogy between geometrical items and numbers. Line segments understood as analogues to numbers form a model for a number system much more extensive than the rationals, that is, the reals, which however is itself marked by an important heterogeneity, segregating rational, algebraic, and irrational numbers. A conflict thus exists between the theory of proportions that Descartes espouses, which tends to restrict the number concept, and the unacknowledged, unarticulated analogy which his choice of line segments as terms sets up, which tends to lay the number concept wide open. But Descartes never explores this tension, because it entails a heterogeneity between numbers and lines, which his method cannot admit. In fact, his method conflates them, and then the interest of the analogy is obscured. Leibniz, not Descartes, is the mathematician who recognizes the importance of irrational numbers.

Moreover, when terms are not allowed to maintain their stubborn differences, they are wholly subordinated to the ratios which bind them. A significant distinction remains in the classical tradition between terms and ratios, whereas in the medieval tradition ratios like terms are just numbers. Leibniz's ability to think of relations as virtual, not actually completed operations, distinct from the terms they link, allows him to legitimize the introduction of infinitesimals into mathematics and mathematical physics, where they prove indispensable. But such strategies of generalization are out of the question for Descartes.

I said earlier that my second quarrel with Descartes is that he misses the import of his abstract relational structure. The abstract rational structure of the *Geometry* is given not only by a tacit theory of proportions, but also by an algebra presented on the first few pages of Book I. It consists of expressions involving known $(a,b,...)$ and unknown $(x,y,...)$ quantities, connected by (only finitely iterated) addition, subtraction, multiplication, division, and nth root signs, and equated to each other by equals signs. The algebra of arithmetic which Descartes has inherited from the tradition and improved by some new notation tells him what are well-formed expressions ($\sqrt{(a^2+b^2)}$), true equations ($-az+b^2=b^2-az$), and sound inferences from one equation to another (if $z^2=az+b^2$ then $z=\frac{1}{2}a+\sqrt{(\frac{1}{4}a^2+b^2)}$), on the basis of what holds true for relations among integers.[43]

Recall that in the *Discourse on Method* Descartes says of algebra only that it serves as a shorthand and bookkeeping device for geometric reasonings about proportions: 'I considered, however, that in order to keep them in my memory or to embrace several at once, it would be essential that I should explain them by means of certain formulas, the shorter the better.'[44] Just as a theory of proportions has no explicit place in the order of reasons of the *Geometry*, still less so does the algebra of arithmetic. Descartes never thinks of algebra as a source of mathematical knowledge, items, or problems; he never introduces a curve, for instance, by means of the algebraic equation alone. So too he never wonders what might be the consequences of changing from a mathematical idiom of proportions to one of algebraic equations, or what might happen to algebra when its domain is line segments (and curves and surfaces and so forth) rather than integers.

Descartes's methodology leads him to view geometry as the construction of increasingly complex entities out of homogeneous, place-holder starting-points by means of association, proportions, which are transparent to reason. In fact, I want to argue, he has two relational structures at work (a theory of proportions and an algebra) which allow him to relate by analogy a domain of number and a domain of geometrical entities. His method therefore suppresses a whole host of questions which will prove significant for mathematical research: Where do the two abstract structures come from? Are they equivalent? Do they themselves contain obscurities? How are they justified? How might they be modified? Since they can be applied to both number and space, does the induced analogy change those domains, and might that change rebound on the abstract structures?

I have argued in the first section of this chapter that Descartes's commitment to his homogeneous starting-points, line segments, and to the reductive claims of his method to exfoliate a whole subject-matter out of those starting-points prevents him from being able to focus his mathematical attention on curves as such. Now I want to argue further that his tendency to conflate numerical and geometric entities as place-holders in an unexamined abstract structure prevents him from seeing the real interest of the study of curves which his *Geometry* makes possible. For he cannot see that it produces a novel interaction among the domains of number and geometry, as well as algebra, which becomes a new subject-matter in its own right. And this interaction makes possible the investigation of curves in multivalent but not entirely equivalent and thus immensely suggestive ways: curves can be thought of as spatially shaped entities, as algebraic equations and as courses of (real) number-pairs. By contrast, Leibniz's ability to hold in the tension of analogy these three modes of presentation allows him to begin work on the calculus, with its attendant expansion of the domain of curves, the domain of number, methods of studying the properties of curves, and even the expressive means of algebra itself.[45] It would not be fair to demand of Descartes that he foresee all these developments; but he might be reproached for foreclosing on them ahead of time due to his conception of method.

Notes

1. *La Géométrie*, pp. 40–1, 388.
2. Apropos Descartes's view of algebra, see ch. 6, 'Géométrisme Cartesien et Arithmétisme Leibnizien' in Belaval's *Leibniz critique de Descartes*. See also Bos, 'On the Representation of Curves in Descartes' *Géométrie*', pp. 308 f; and M. Mahoney, 'The Beginnings of Algebraic Thought in the Seventeenth Century' in Gaukroger (ed.), *Descartes: Philosophy, Mathematics and Physics*, pp. 141–55.
3. Bos, 'Representation of Curves in Descartes', pp. 326–30.
4. Ibid. 303.
5. Ibid. 303.
6. *La Géométrie*, pp. 238–41, 485.
7. Ibid. 90–3, 412.
8. Ibid. 44–9, 391–2.
9. The equation for AF e.g. is $x^8 = a^2(x^2 + y^2)^3$. Ibid. 47.
10. Ibid. 48–9, 392.
11. Bos, 'Representation of Curves in Descartes', p. 326.
12. Ibid. 315–17; *La Géométrie*, pp. 86–9, 410–11.
13. Bos, 'Representation of Curves in Descartes', pp. 332–8.
14. *La Géométrie*, pp.48–9, 392–3.
15. Ibid. 240–1, 485.
16. Ibid. 49–55, 393–4.
17. Ibid. 54–7, 394–5.
18. See Belaval, *Leibniz critique de Descartes*, ch. 1.
19. Bos, 'Representation of Curves in Descartes', p. 313.
20. *La Géométrie*, pp. 56–7, 395–6.
21. Bos, 'Representation of Curves in Descartes', p. 305.
22. *La Géométrie*, pp. 192–5, 463–4.
23. Ibid. 193–219, 464–76.
24. Ibid. 82–7, 408–10.
25. Ibid. 218–39, 476–85.
26. Ibid. 240–1, 485.
27. Smith and Latham mistranslate '*degré plus composé*' here as 'degree'.
28. *La Géométrie*, pp. 94–101, 413–17.
29. Ibid. 114–47, 424–40.
30. Euclid, *Elements*, bk. v, defn. 3, in ii. 114.
31. Ibid., bk. v, defn. 4, in ii. 114.
32. Ibid., bk. I, in i. 153–5.
33. See books Gamma and Zeta of Aristotle, *Physics*, ed. R. Hope (Lincoln: University of Nebraska Press, 1961).

34. Euclid, *Elements*, bk. v, defn. 5, in ii. 114.
35. Sylla, 'Compounding Ratios', pp. 22–6.
36. *La Géométrie*, pp. 4–5, 370.
37. See my two essays on these figures: 'Leibniz' Unification of Geometry with Algebra and Dynamics', and 'Some Uses of Proportion in Newton's *Principia*, bk. ı'.
38. Letter from Debeaune for Roberval, 16 Oct. 1638, in Mersenne, *Correspondance*, ed. M. Tannery (16 vols.; Paris: Presses Universitaires de France, 1933–86), viii. 142–3.
39. My account of this problem is extracted from more detailed expositions in C. Scriba, 'Zur Lösung des 2. Debeauneschen Problems durch Descartes', *Archive for History of Exact Sciences*, 1 (1960–2), 406–19, and in Vuillemin, *Mathématiques et métaphysique chez Descartes*, pp. 11–25.
40. Scriba, 'Lösung des 2. Debeauneschen Problems', pp. 413–14.
41. Ibid. 416–18.
42. See J. Hoffman's 'Über Auftauschen und Behandlung von Differentialgleichungen im 17. Jahrhundert', *Humanismus und Technik*, 15 (1972), 1–40, esp. 13–18.
43. *La Géométrie*, pp. 2–15, 369–76.
44. AT vi. 20; HR i. 93.
45. See my 'Leibniz' Unification of Geometry with Algebra and Dynamics'.

3
Descartes's *Principles*: Physical Unities

DESCARTES begins the *Principles of Philosophy* with what he calls an abridged version of the argument of the *Meditations*, as if to indicate that his renovated version of physical science, designed as a replacement for outmoded Aristotelianism, was the next stage in the unfolding of the analytic order of reasons that begins with the 'I think' of the first Meditation.[1] Meditations V and VI show how the existence of an infinite, omnipotent, and benevolent God, revealed in the disproportion between the clear and distinct idea of God and the finite human knower, assures the objective truth of mathematical ideas and the possibility of scientific knowledge about the external physical world, quantifiable *res extensa*. Part I of the *Principles* recapitulates these arguments, and then in Part II the three laws of motion are derived from a characterization of God as the primary and immutable cause of motion. In Part III and in scattered passages thereafter, Descartes gives a cosmogony where God as the cause of motion constructs the physical universe according to the analytic order of reasons. This account is only offered as a 'myth', but it mirrors Descartes's intuitionist construction of physical nature as a possible object of human knowledge, a new domain articulated and bounded according to the order of reasons.[2]

Mathematics plays a central role in Descartes's new physics, though, as I shall show in the next three chapters, the threads of his equivocal geometrization of nature are not at all easy to disentangle. Descartes makes a surprising claim in section 11 of Part II of the *Principles of Philosophy*, suggesting that there is no difference, but only a difference of thought, between the subject-matter of geometry and that of physics.

If we concentrate on the idea which we have of some body, for example a stone, and remove from that idea everything which we know is not essential to the nature of body; we shall easily understand that the same extension which constitutes the nature of body also constitutes the nature of space, and that these two things differ only in the way that the nature of the genus or species differs from that of the individual.[3]

It is certainly true that mathematics is not about true individuals, only genera or, as we might say now, equivalence classes. Descartes suggests that individuals which instantiate geometrical forms are what physics is about. *Res extensa* thus becomes the principle of individuation of the external world; the book of nature might be written in mathematics, but matter is what makes it an indefinite collection of separate things, each taking up its own place in the larger order. Moreover, nothing more can be said about the essence of *res extensa* than that it instantiates geometrical forms. It is purely homogeneous extendedness, and so it has no other essential qualities.

But to move from geometry to physics, Descartes requires not only matter but motion. The linkage between Parts I and II of the *Principles* presents God as the seat of motion: He injects and conserves it in the physical world. In Cartesian metaphysics, passive and inert matter is radically distinguished from active spirit, and so helps to keep the creation separate from God and Descartes safe from the pantheistic heresy that was to endanger Spinoza. Is motion then part of the essence of matter? This is a hard question to answer, and has sparked controversy among scholars; I will return to it later.[4] At this stage I only want to point out that matter as the subject of physics apparently cannot be characterized apart from geometry and God.

The clear and simple starting-points which Descartes should easily be able to discover for the commencement of his physics thus turn out to be somewhat elusive. In one sense the starting-point of the *Principles* is *res extensa* taken as a whole, opposed to God and man as radically different in kind and perhaps not even possessed of geometric structure. In another sense it is the simplex out of which God generates the world: a bit of matter in rectilinear, uniform (unaccelerated) motion. My intention in the first section of this chapter is to exhibit the trouble this ambiguity generates for Descartes, even as he explicitly chooses the latter version, whose strengths and weaknesses I examine in the second section. It allows Descartes to break with the Aristotelian dogma that there are five distinct kinds of matter, each with a different kind of associated motion. But when these starting-points are fed into his reductive method, homogeneity is so strictly asserted and terms so strongly subordinated to relations, that Descartes has difficulty accounting for the stability, integrity, and persistence of material objects.

He also has a hard time reinstating the material diversity he needs to give a mechanist model of the cosmos. In Chapter 4 I continue my examination of these themes in the context of Descartes's laws of motion. This chapter and the next are designed to show how Descartes's methodological assumptions at once help him to envisage a new physics, and impair his ability to develop it. That starting-points are simple and easy to find, that they are mere place-holders in abstract relational structures which exhaust them, that diverse, stable complexity can be introduced and reliably extrapolated by means of these structures which are transparent to reason, and that distinct domains can be related by a kind of conflation of subject-matters under the aegis of these structures: all these assumptions that we recognize as at work in the *Geometry* are also at work in the *Principles*, with many of the same consequences. Chapter 5 goes on to explore in detail the difficulties Cartesian reduction poses for the application of mathematics to various processes and problems in natural science.

LOCATING THE STARTING-POINTS

Res extensa lends itself to being organized by the method and thus becoming a scientific subject-matter because it is quantifiable; Descartes claims that *res extensa* differs from three-dimensional Euclidean space only as the genus or species differs from the individual. Apparently Descartes can organize the *Principles* because God has already organized the world; but how was God able to organize the world? Did He confer geometric structure on *res extensa*, or did *res extensa* already have it? Without the active interference of God, injecting a constant amount of motion in diversely distributed increments throughout its extent, would *res extensa* have any intelligible structure at all?

In a letter to Henry More, Descartes writes, 'I hold that if matter is left to itself and receives no external impulse it will remain perfectly quiescent.'[5] This passage indicates that for Descartes there is at least an analysable moment in the concept of the substance *res extensa* where it can be considered independent of God's injection of motion into it. And the cosmogony in Part III of the *Principles* yields a genetic version, as if there were a stage in the career of matter temporally prior to God's injection of motion.

Let us suppose, if you please, that God, in the beginning, divided all the matter of which he formed the visible world into parts as equal as possible and of medium size, that is to say that their size was the average of all the various sizes of the parts which now compose the heavens and the stars. And let us suppose that he endowed them collectively with exactly the amount of motion which is still in the world at present.[6]

In this cosmological context, the true seat of all activity or force is God, since matter is taken to be passive and inert apart from God's action upon it. Motion is a mode of matter, but the cause and origin of motion is God, for activity must be referred to spirit. Thus, we should look closely at the stage of *res extensa* when it is 'perfectly quiescent', for this stage reveals important aspects of and difficulties involved in its concept.

Descartes takes quiescent *res extensa* to be a plenum of homogeneous stuff, three dimensional and indefinite in extent. These features are explicated in sections 4-23 of Part II of the *Principles*, which treat *res extensa* in itself; the explication of motion begins at section 23.[7] Each feature is asserted on analogy with three-dimensional Euclidean space, which has no holes, is perfectly symmetric and isotropic, and has no boundaries. In the *Geometry*, Descartes's method sometimes leads to the collapse of analogies into (alleged) identities. Just as it conflates the domains of number and geometry, here it conflates geometry and physics, as if the differences between their subject-matters were negligible in view of the abstract relational structure they share.

Descartes derives his denial of the void from the identity of three-dimensional Euclidean space with *res extensa;* the world is a plenum and physical space is mathematical space.

11. We may take away cold, heat, and all other properties which are either not considered to be always in the stone, or which could be changed without the stone being thought to have lost the nature of body. For then we shall clearly notice that absolutely nothing remains in our idea of the stone except that (we distinctly perceive that) it is something extended in length, breadth, and depth; and this fact is also included in our idea of space, and not only of space which is full of bodies, but also of space which is called a void.

12. How space differs from material substance in the way in which it is conceived. There is however a difference in our way of conceiving them; for when a stone has been removed from the space or place in which it was, we think that its extension has also been removed; since we regard that

extension as unique and inseparable from the body. However, we judge that the extension of the place in which the stone was remains and is the same, although the stone's place may now be occupied by wood, or water, or air, or any other body; or may even be believed to be empty. The reason for this is that extension in that case is being considered in a general way.[8]

The only difference between geometrical and physical space which Descartes is willing to admit is that between genus or species and its individual instantiation. Note that in the passage above Descartes only discusses the case of a finite part of matter (a stone) and its extension; but for consistency's sake, the identity should apply as well to the great monolith of *res extensa*. Thus it appears that quiescent *res extensa* is a material instantiation of three-dimensional Euclidean space taken as a whole, which exhibits exactly the same features as its 'genus'. But what kind of unity and what kind of internal organization, if any, does it have? Is it a possible object of knowledge? Could it serve as the starting point of a science?

In order to answer these questions about quiescent *res extensa*, we need to look at the answers to them in the case of three-dimensional Euclidean space. Though it does not have any external boundaries, three-dimensional Euclidean space has an internal articulation which stems from the way in which points bound lines, lines bound surfaces, and surfaces bound volumes. We have seen that Descartes was not much interested in these bounding relationships and the unities they involve, though he exploits them when he needs to;[9] this casual exploitation occurs in the *Principles* as well as in the *Geometry*. But in classical mathematics, the study of such relationships and unities reveals the features of Euclidean space itself, its lack of holes, its homogeneity and its indefinite extent. (One might also add, in anachronistic topological terms, its connectedness: Euclidean space is all of a piece, and does not fall apart into two or more distinct segments.) Points, line segments, shaped areas, and volumes are the parts of Euclidean space and also, as boundaries, determine its parts; and this internal articulation of Euclidean space into parts both determines, and is determined by, the features of Euclidean space as a partless whole.

For in one sense, three-dimensional Euclidean space as a whole does not have parts: one region is not distinguishable from another precisely because Euclidean space is symmetric and isotropic, does not have holes or boundaries, and is not disconnected. One might want to call it a unity simply in virtue of the fact that it has no parts.[10]

Euclidean space itself certainly does not have that kind of unity conferred by shape, that of a cube or a sphere for example; it is 'indefinite in extent'. If it did have the unity of shape, it would also have to have parts in the sense of distinguishable regions. The kind of unity which Euclidean space as a whole enjoys requires partlessness and boundlessness, and so is quite unlike the unity of shape, which depends on the way in which some geometric objects bound, and serve as components of, others.

But in another sense, three-dimensional Euclidean space does have parts, the internal articulation and organization provided by points, bounded lines, surfaces, and volumes. And these parts both condition and are conditioned by the partless unity which Euclidean space as a whole exhibits. Euclidean space is a possible object of knowledge because of the mutual determination of its internal articulation into parts (some of which themselves have a characteristic unity, the unity of shape) and its partless unity as a whole.

What about the case of *res extensa*? Descartes implies that quiescent *res extensa* would be quite like three-dimensional Euclidean space in so far as it also seems to exhibit a partless, regionless unity as a whole: isotropic, symmetric, connected, no holes or external boundaries. It would be a great indeterminate rigid body, an unbounded monolith. However, he also implies that it has so far no internal articulation, because in quiescent *res extensa* there is no physical analogue of a boundary, and so consequently, of a point, bounded line, surface, or volume. There are no articulating parts which themselves have the integrity of shape. But if the internal articulation into parts of Euclidean space is the condition for the partless, regionless unity as a whole which it exhibits, one must wonder on what grounds Descartes assumes that he can know what quiescent *res extensa* would be like, with an analogous partless, regionless unity. Without internal organization, *res extensa* is not a possible object of knowledge and has no structure. It is a surd, and Descartes has no warrant to make any claims about its characteristics.

Descartes's method forces him into an interesting dilemma here. On the one hand, it suggests a strong analogy verging on identity between mathematical space and *res extensa*; Descartes hopes to build a new quantified science of nature upon the recognition of their shared relational structure. In so far as quiescent *res extensa* is a plausible candidate for the material instantiation of three-dimensional Euclidean space, it should have inherent geometrical structure. On the other hand, Cartesian method requires adequate starting-points which are moreover simple and easy to understand. To the degree that Descartes wishes to locate such starting-points for physics, he must enrich his model of *res extensa* in such a way that its disanalogies with geometrical space are admitted and even exacerbated. Physical boundaries and hence physical unities require God's injection of motion into the great monolith of quiescent *res extensa*. But then apparently the latter has no inherent geometrical structure, if a physical geometry is intended. (Moreover, the internal articulation of the plenum which results from the injection of motion is quite unlike that of Descartes's geometry and indeed in many respects is incompatible with it; I will return to this point in Chapters 4 and 5.)

Does quiescent *res extensa* have geometrical structure, or does it not? This question is difficult to answer, not only for the reasons just cited, but because of the ambiguity in Descartes's handling of geometry. No dualist can leave his polar terms wholly sundered if he is going to address the problem of human knowledge or found a science of physics. Descartes certainly cannot, especially since his method, with its insistence on homogeneity and simplicity, reveals that he has the instincts of a monist. As I will argue at greater length in Chapter 7, Descartes engages a variety of middle terms in order to assimilate matter and spirit, and one of them is geometry. It does not clearly belong to either category, and the ambiguity of its ontological classification allows Descartes to use it as a bridge.

Geometry seems to belong to the category of spirit at the beginning of the *Meditations*, and of its recapitulation in Part I of the *Principles*.[11] For there the self in its first person perspective is furnished with the ideas of its own self-consciousness, God, and mathematics, ideas which are secured for it independent of whether or not the material world, *res extensa*, exists. But geometry seems to belong to the category of matter in the passages cited above from sections 11 and 12 of Part II, where Descartes claims that Euclidean space does not differ from material substance. Geometry, a purely intelligible structure which is none the less instantiated by matter, links mind to matter and supplies the possibility of our knowledge of the external world; this is the lesson of Meditation VI. The question whether quiescent *res extensa* has geometric structure intrinsically or only in virtue of the activity of God is a version of the question, is the category for geometry matter or spirit?

One way or the other, quiescent *res extensa* is not going to provide the requisite starting-point for Descartes's physics unless it can be individuated, broken up into bits which can serve as the place-holders for his abstract relational structure. How shall such bits be constituted? What should count as one bit? According to what criteria should its unity be asserted?

In some passages Descartes writes as if matter were individuated and boundaries formed within the monolith of quiescent *res extensa* solely in virtue of motion whose cause is God's activity or force. A division within matter occurs only when some parts of matter move, however slightly, with respect to other parts of matter. Descartes introduces the topic of motion into his discussion of *res extensa* in Part II of the *Principles* explicitly at section 23. There he says that since *res extensa* is in itself homogeneous, all its diversity must be referred to motion. 'For although our minds can imagine divisions (in that matter), this (imagining) alone cannot change matter in any way; rather, all the variation of matter, or all the diversity of its forms, depends on motion.'[12] If Descartes constituting this new subject-matter is identified with God in the process of constructing the world, one might conclude from this passage that God can only realize a geometric structure of shaped volumes within *res extensa* by injecting motion into it.

Two sections later, in 25, Descartes first defines motion as 'the transference of one part of matter or of one body, from the vicinity of those bodies immediately contiguous to it and considered as at rest, into the vicinity of (some) others.' He then goes on to define one body, or one part of matter, as 'everything which is simultaneously transported; even though this may be composed of many parts which have other movements among themselves.'[13] What is considered one part of matter may, indeed must, itself have parts, each of which will have its own characterizing motion that is then combined (by a sort of vectorial addition) with the motion of the whole, which it shares with the other parts. One part of matter must have parts because that is how its unity is defined, by the common motion of its parts.

This definition of 'one part of matter' allows for some very peculiar entities, since it does not require that the parts be contiguous, only that they share a common motion. A flock of particles

Descartes's Principles: Physical Unities

dispersed over the whole solar system might count as one part of matter, if at least one vectorial component of the motion of each could be identified as in the same equivalence class (to use modern terminology.) Descartes's discussion of rarefaction at the beginning of Part II suggests that he would like to be able to consider slightly dispersed collections as one thing.[14] But in general his discussion seems orientated towards rigid, solid bodies, of the kind that the original individuation of *res extensa* by God would produce. Descartes's definition of solid bodies, given in sections 54 and 55 of Part II, adds the further condition that the parts of solid bodies are contiguous and at rest with respect to each other.[15] The latter section is particularly noteworthy.

55. That the parts of solid bodies are not joined by any other bonds than their own rest (relative to each other). Furthermore, our reason certainly cannot discover any bond which could join the particles of solid bodies more firmly together than does their own rest. For what could this bond be? It could not be a substance, because there is no reason why these particles, which are substances, should be joined by any substance other than themselves. Nor is it a mode different from rest; for no other mode can be more opposed to the movement which would separate these particles than is their own rest. Yet, besides substances and modes, we know no other kinds of things.[16]

Here Descartes invokes the first law of motion (section 37), which says that each thing, as far as is in its power, always remains in the same state.[17] A solid body which is, for example, a sphere will tend to retain that shape. And yet its persistence as one thing, Descartes makes clear, has nothing to do with its shape. For shape is a mode of matter which Descartes explicitly eliminates here; the persistence of the part's parts as one thing can only be explained by appeal to their mutual rest. In sum, geometrical shape cannot serve as a principle of individuation for *res extensa*; Descartes requires a principle which is physical and indeed kinetic (and perhaps dynamic). As I argued earlier, matter is after all supposed to be a principle of individuation for the genera of mathematics.

However, with this definition of the unity of a physical body as common motion of parts, Descartes has created a problem of circularity for himself as constitutor of physics. For he must assume that parts of matter are already available to be associated by a common motion to form a physical whole, 'one part of matter'. If these parts are kinematically individuated, then he has presupposed the very individuation he sought to explain. If not, then they are available as material parts solely in virtue of their geometric shape, a geometric articulation that must belong to *res extensa* intrinsically. But this is an alternative Descartes has denied.

Descartes's definition of motion also involves an appeal to parts of matter as already available. Epistemically, this means that motion can be identified as such only when one already has prior access to knowledge of what counts as a material unity, knowledge which itself depends on the identification of common motion. Genetically, this means that while motion requires available parts (for certainly the monolith of inert *res extensa* cannot be moved), the availability of parts *qua* individuated matter requires motion. These difficulties resemble the problems of circularity apropos the construction of line segments in the beginning of the *Geometry* in a deep way, for they stem from Cartesian method's demand for simple and radically primary starting-points, and its subordination of the simples to the abstract relational structure in which they stand.

All that can save Descartes from such circularities in his physics is the prior geometric articulation of quiescent *res extensa*. And indeed sometimes Descartes writes as if this kind of individuation were allowable after all, especially in passages before Part II, section 23, where motion is introduced. In such passages, not surprisingly, he assimilates *res extensa* most closely to mathematical extension. In section 13 he writes, 'For in fact the names "place" or "space" do not signify a thing different from the body which is said to be in the place; but only designate its size, shape and situation among other bodies.'[18] And in section 16, in one of his arguments against the void, he says, 'From the sole fact that a body is extended in length, breadth and depth, we rightly conclude that it is a substance.'[19] Descartes assumes here that what makes a physical object one thing is that it exists as a shaped volume, for he has as yet said nothing about the differentiated motion which creates boundaries; the boundaries he invokes are purely geometric.

Descartes wants both to deny and to assert an internal articulation, a geometric organization, of inert *res extensa* prior to the divine injection of motion which orders and individuates it. On the one hand, he realizes that a science of nature requires principles of individuation which are distinctively kinematic or dynamic. The merely formal unities of geometry will not suffice to create the starting-points of physics out of the monolith of inert *res extensa*.

Descartes's Principles: Physical Unities

Moreover, his radical dualism tends to push all unity, activity, and intelligibility over towards the category of spirit. Inert *res extensa* is shorn of cognitive structure and God is made to account for the ways in which matter is accessible to the human mind as the subject-matter of a science. Divine motion then provides the internal articulation of *res extensa*.

On the other hand, Descartes is also tempted to say that *res extensa* in itself, prior to God's intervention, does have a purely geometric structure. He needs some kind of articulation of *res extensa* to underwrite the prior availability of parts which then, aggregated by common motion, constitute physical unities. More generally, he needs some way of rescuing *res extensa* from the consequences of his radical dualism. The transfer of unity, activity, and intelligibility to the side of spirit reduces matter to such a surd that it becomes unclear how *res extensa* could figure in a science or lend itself to God's organizing activity in the first place. Descartes's identification of *res extensa* with three-dimensional Euclidean space and all its rich structure provides a kind of prior template on which God and Descartes the constitutor of physics can then act.

The complexity and inconsistency of Descartes's discussion of *res extensa* in Part II of the *Principles* indicates that it is not in fact always easy for him to locate starting-points for a discipline. Descartes is not sure whether his starting-points are geometric or kinematic (or dynamic). Nor is he sure where to refer the origins of the intelligibly complex structure of matter whose simples his method enjoins him to identify. God alone, inert *res extensa*, or pure geometry are all unsuitable for providing physics with a starting-point. The most plausible candidate is an uneasy compound of the three: a bit of matter which is a shaped volume, individuated and set in rectilinear, uniform motion by God. In the sections that follow, I will examine how Cartesian method both fosters and thwarts the development of a science from this starting-point.

CONSTITUTING PHYSICAL OBJECTS

Descartes begins the *Geometry* with the 'clear and simple' starting-points of finite rectilinear line segments, which are then associated by 'rational relations' into entities of higher complexity, notably problems and secondarily curves. In the last two chapters I argued that Descartes does not find the characteristic unity of line segments or curves worthy of discussion; that he uses two non-equivalent relational structures; that he has difficulty establishing a hierarchy of distinct kinds of problems and curves because his reductionism tends to pull the complexes back to the simples and his faith in the transparency of rational relations leads him to rash generalization; and that he often brings complexity in by the back door to enrich the domain which he has impoverished by his insistence on homogeneity and the subordination of terms to relations. And so his method hampers the development of his algebraized geometry, which none the less streamlines and unifies classical mathematics in useful ways.

In the *Principles*, Descartes cannot ignore the issue of how the integrity of his starting-points is to be constituted. Because the origins of *res extensa* are tied up with God and geometry, Descartes's ultimate choice of bits of matter in rectilinear uniform motion requires some prior sorting out of other possible starting-points. Section 25 of Part II contains the sharpest formulation of how Descartes conceives of these starting-points. Motion is 'the transference of one part of matter or of one body, from the vicinity of those bodies immediately contiguous to it and considered as at rest, into the vicinity of (some) others.' And one body or 'one part of matter' is defined as 'everything which is simultaneously transported, even though this may be composed of many parts which have other movements among themselves'. A motion must be referred to something which counts as one body; and one body as such has only one motion.[20]

The great virtue of these definitions is that they free Descartes from the Aristotelian distinctions among earth, water, fire, air, and ether, each element with its own distinctive kind of motion, and the concomitant assumption that sublunary and superlunary nature must be treated as two separate sciences. The drift of Cartesian method is to integrate domains. All the matter in the whole universe is of one and the same kind; all movement is of itself along straight lines; all material interactions are collisions between particles. With these assumptions, physics and astronomy are subsumed under the same laws. The vision of science thus unified ushers in a new era.

The starting-points of Descartes's physics, however, prove to be problematic. Their characteristic unity is unsatisfactory, because the simples keep dispersing into a system of abstract relations. Once again, two distinct kinds of relational structure can be identified.

Descartes's Principles: Physical Unities

The establishment of an articulated hierarchy of complexes within physics turns out to be very difficult. Finally, the impoverishment of Descartes's geometry also affects his science. I will deal immediately with the first point, and take up the other points in Chapters 4 and 5.

It is well known that Descartes's definitions of place and motion are relativistic. Where a body is and how it is moving are definable only with respect to the configuration of other bodies in its vicinity.

13. What external place is. For in fact the names 'place' or 'space' do not signify a thing different from the body which is said to be in the place; but only designate its size, shape and situation among other bodies.[21]

28. That movement, properly understood, concerns only the bodies contiguous to the body which is moving.[22]

The system of relative positions defining place and motion, identified with Euclidean geometry, constitutes the first set of rational relations which associate physical simples, bits of matter in uniform, rectilinear motion.

A collection of parts is one thing, according to Descartes, only if its parts share a common motion. Thus, its unity is independent of what shape, size, or speed it has; and there are no degrees of unity. A large, slow sphere is just as much one thing as a small, fast cube, as long as its parts share a common motion. And a collection of parts which almost but does not quite share a common motion does not meet the criterion of unity. However slight a differentiating movement, Descartes says, it is nevertheless a true division.

34. All the particles into which one can imagine such a unit of matter to be divisible, and which are truly innumerable, must move slightly with respect to one another; and however slight this movement, it is nevertheless a true division.[23]

Does a simple in Descartes's physics have parts or does it not? Either way his model of matter gets into trouble. If it does not have parts, then its unity is forfeited, for the unity of a physical thing is defined as 'common motion of parts'. If it has virtual parts, then Descartes is thrown back on the individuation of matter by geometry alone, as a shaped volume. This must be the case in his definition of a solid body, where he claims the parts are contiguous and at rest with respect to each other (as at the same time they share their common motion). These parts are not therefore parts in a kinematic, but only a geometric sense. Unless Descartes wants to accept geometrically individuated parts, virtual parts, he is left with a simple which is one because of its partlessness, a kind of unity which is reserved for spirit and would moreover be incompatible with his rejection of atoms.

If the body has parts which are kinematically individuated, then each part must have its own peculiar motion, as well as the motion it shares with the other parts in order to constitute 'one thing'. The motion of this part will then be the kind of compound motion Descartes illustrates by a diagram, one of the very few in the *Principles* which looks anything at all like those in the *Geometry* (Fig. 3.1).[24] The compound motion will be something like the vectorial sum of the two motions, although it is anachronistic to speak of vectors in the context of Cartesian physics. In addition, to avoid the threat of atoms or purely geometric individuation, each part must have its subparts, each subpart its own sub-subparts, and so on indefinitely. The result of all this is a swarm of indefinitely small parts, each with its own distinct trajectory; the 'unity' of this swarm is that each particle-trajectory has one (out of 'indefinitely many' others) vectorial component which lies in the same equivalence class with one component of the trajectories of each of the other particles. This is a fairly pallid kind of unity, especially since these particles do not even have to touch or lie close to each other to constitute 'one thing'. In this snowstorm of particles, no one could identify the 'things' except perhaps God, who knows a priori what He intended to exist as unities.

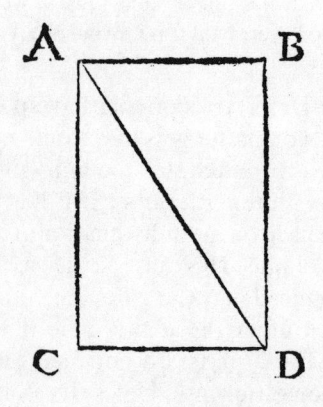

Fig. 3.1

The foregoing considerations perhaps did not occur to Descartes since he was probably thinking of mid-range objects composed of particles relatively close to and almost at rest with respect to each other, and much smaller by many orders of magnitude than the objects themselves. Still, either Descartes must then invoke particles of infinitesimal size and motion (so that their deviations are negligible), or such mid-range objects, which are almost solids, reveal even deeper difficulties in Descartes's criterion of unity. In section 54, just after his exposition of the seven rules of impact, Descartes defines solid and fluid bodies this way: 'those bodies which are divided into very small parts which are agitated by a diversity of (independent) movements, are fluid; while those bodies whose particles are all contiguous and at rest, are solid.'[25]

My criticism of Descartes's criterion of unity here echoes Leibniz's frequent complaint that Descartes did not honour the principle of continuity. The case of rest ought to be a limiting case for slower and slower motion, especially since Descartes recognized something like the concept of an inertial frame, which his follower Huygens took over and used to such scientifically acute ends. But consider the case of Descartes's hypothetical quasi-solid. If it is at rest, its parts are at rest with respect to each other except for each one's own small characteristic deviating motion; but then since the common vectorial component is zero, the actual motion is that each part is moving off on its own, and the alleged solid looks like a liquid. Indeed, it does not even look like one thing, since there is no common motion. When do we refer to liquids as 'one thing'? Generally, for example in the case of a pond, when they are held within a container which is itself a solid. But the unity imposed by a container on a liquid is accidental, not the sort of thing that a science of physics would study in investigating the integrity of its starting-points.[26]

What if we change the inertial frame of this puzzling entity, the hypothetical quasi-solid, so that it moves at a constant velocity and thus its parts share a common motion? Now it seems to qualify as 'one thing'. But why should a change of inertial frame affect the unity of a physical object, so that in this frame 'it' is not one, but in that frame it is? This drastic change violates the principle of continuity. Moreover, the entity, though now qualifying as one thing, still looks like a liquid, in this case a river whose 'small parts are agitated by a diversity of independent movements' even though they are all flowing to the sea. Then the problem of the container reasserts itself. Under none of these construals does Descartes's definition offer a convincing model of physical unity.

All these difficulties, I suggest, have their origin in Descartes's reductive method, which insists that beginning points serve merely as homogeneous place-holders in the relational structure which they instantiate. In the *Geometry*, Descartes does not stop to examine his starting-points—line segments—for this very reason. He assumes that they have no integrity of their own worth investigating beyond what he can learn from the rational relations they enter into. And since he treats the relational structure as fixed, he cannot entertain the possibility of interesting heterogeneity in the terms, which might force a revision of the relational structure. In the *Principles*, because it is clear that the purely geometric unity of shape is not going to suffice for the constitution of physical unities, Descartes must give an account of the kind of integrity which his starting-points have. But his account takes away the very integrity it is supposed to introduce: the whole is not greater than the sum of its parts, and there is no systematic interdependency among the parts, or among the parts and the whole.

Cartesian method on the one hand enjoins that complex unities must be (no more than) rational relations among simples; thus the complexes tend to be reduced to, to crumble into, the simples. The simples are what 'really' exists for intuition. But what is a simple? As soon as it is granted any characteristics, that is, an internal articulation, it becomes a congeries of further simples. On the other hand, the simples are described as being merely place-holders within a system of rational relations, which captures all that is important about them. Thus, if an account of the integrity of a simple is to be given, it must be given in terms of the system of rational relations. In the case of bits of matter, the relevant system of rational relations is the system given by Euclidean geometry. Thus the integrity of the starting-point, the simple, the place-holder, dissolves into the system of rational relations. 'One part of matter' becomes nothing but a system of common motion . . . of what? Of parts which are themselves no more than systems of common motion, *ad infinitum*.

The great complex unities of the world dissolve into simples which dissolve into relations of relations *ad infinitum*. Cartesian method allows no place for the reflective examination of the charac-

Descartes's Principles: Physical Unities

teristic kinds of unities that found subject-matters, or, when such examination is unavoidable, offers an illusory appeal to a system of relations which requires for its own intelligibility but cannot furnish by itself the sought-for account. The circularity here deserves the adjective 'vicious', and exemplifies one of the real metaphysical weaknesses of Descartes's philosophy.

In the next chapter, I will examine the consequences of the evanescent, unstable unity of Descartes's physical simples in the context of his laws of motion, which introduce a second, distinct system of rational relations, colliding bodies that conserve something like momentum. The instability of the simples will work against Descartes's attempt to establish vortices as high-level complex unities, and to differentiate matter into three elements. In Chapter 5, I will trace out and explain the difficulties Descartes has in mathematizing his physics thus constituted. And in Chapter 6, I will turn to Descartes's attempt to reconstruct the even higher-level complex unities, living organisms, in terms of his physics. As in geometry, so here Descartes's most interesting inventions often occur when he violates the stricture of his own method. Conversely, his method, deployed in full force, tends to reduce nature to the ghostly dust of relation.

Notes

1. Some scholars, including Gueroult, read the *Principles* as ordered synthetically, not analytically. But, as Garber and Cohen argue in 'A Point of Order: Analysis, Synthesis, and Descartes' *Principles*', the textual support for such a claim is scant, based mostly on a passage from the *Conversations with Burman* (AT v. 153). They refrain from claiming that the *Principles* is thus arranged according to the analytic order of reasons, but I hope my commentary will persuade the reader that it is. For a careful discussion of how Descartes's metaphysical claims are related to the first principles of his physics, see Clarke, *Descartes' Philosophy of Science*, ch. 4.
2. The *Principia Philosophiae* was originally published in Latin in Amsterdam in 1644, and then translated into French by Picot in 1647; Descartes oversaw the translation. I use the English translation given in the *Principles of Philosophy,* ed. V. R. Miller and R. P. Miller (Dordrecht: D. Reidel, 1983–4), where passages in parentheses represent material interpolated at this later stage. For each citation, I will give first the page numbers in Miller and Miller and then the page numbers from vol. viii. 1–348 of Adam and Tannery, where the *Principles* is reprinted: in this case, 105–8; 99–103.
3. *Principia Philosophiae*, pp. 44; 46.
4. See D. Garber, 'Mind, Body and the Laws of Nature', *Midwest Studies in Philosophy*, 8 (1983), 105–33; as well as Gabbey, 'Force and Inertia in the Seventeenth Century: Descartes and Newton' in *Descartes: Philosophy, Mathematics and Physics.*
5. Descartes, *Correspondance*, ed. C. Adam and G. Milhaud (8 vols.; Paris: Félix Alcan, 1936), viii. 261–7. Descartes to More, Aug. 1649. I will refer to this edition as AM, followed by volume and page number; the English translations are my own.
6. *Principia Philosophiae*, pp. 106–7; 100–1.
7. Ibid. 40–50; 42–53.
8. Ibid. 44–5; 46–7.
9. Descartes's preoccupation with a closed algebra of line segments precludes his interest in such problems. He does mention once that equations can correspond to surfaces as well as curves, but he does not develop this observation; *La Géométrie*, pp. 80–1; 407.
10. Thus this space metaphorically resembles spirit; Henry More and Newton were both attracted by this likeness.
11. *Principia Philosophiae*, pp. 3–36; 5–39.
12. Ibid. 50; 52–3.

13. Ibid. 51; 53–4.
14. Ibid. 41–2; 42–4.
15. Ibid. 69–70; 70–1.
16. Ibid. 70; 71.
17. Ibid. 59; 62–3.
18. Ibid. 45; 47.
19. Ibid. 46–7; 49.
20. Ibid. 51; 53–4.
21. Ibid. 45; 47.
22. Ibid. 52; 55.
23. Ibid. 56–7; 59–60.
24. Ibid. 289; 58. See also sects. 31 and 32 of Pt. II, to which the diagram refers, pp. 54–5; 57–8.
25. Ibid. 69–70; 70–1.
26. I owe this insight to a conversation with Dudley Shapere.

4
Laws of Motion

IN Part II of the *Principles*, Descartes wants to characterize the motion of the interaction between parts of matter by means of his three laws of motion, the third of which consists of seven rules governing collisions between bits of matter. These laws set up a second system of rational relations among bits of matter, whose classical antecedent is not Euclidean geometry, but the theory of simple machines as presented in the *Mechanical Questions* attributed to Aristotle, and the *Mechanics* of Heron of Alexandria. Galileo and Torricelli, like da Vinci before them, study the phenomena of percussion or impact as analogous to the scales, the lever, the pulley, and the screw, that is, as requiring a mathematical analysis in terms of an invariant which characterizes the state of equilibrium. Every mechanical effect can be represented as an equilibrium between two equal products, the product of weight times velocity, which Galileo calls 'momento'.[1] Descartes takes over from this tradition his third law of motion, although as usual he acknowledges no debt to tradition, only to his own innate ideas. The third law constitutes *res extensa* as an indefinitely large system of colliding particles in whose interactions an invariant is conserved.

The new relational structure, though mathematical, belongs to mechanics, not geometry; it is simply not shared by the objects of geometry. And so Descartes's original simples, defined by common motion, prove to have an integrity inadequate for the structure; they are literally too friable, and the structure threatens to reduce them to structureless 'subtle matter'. Descartes has two ways of handling this problem, both of which violate the requirements of his reductive method. First, he temporarily abstracts from the divisibility of his simples, and treats them like atoms in his presentation of the rules of impact. Secondly, he admits their divisibility later just at the point when he is conferring a sort of unity on them by a condition stronger than mere common motion in order to differentiate them into three kinds. In this case I will argue that he is not entitled to his invocation of shape, size, and speed as factors affecting the stability and segregation of bits of matter, nor to the external factors of impacting bodies and shaping containers. An interesting disparity between the first and second relational structures, as Descartes tacitly shifts from geometry to mechanics, forces a shift away from the simples as originally defined. Cartesian method is supposed to preclude such interaction between relational structure and simples, or revision of the simples; but Descartes goes ahead with his tacit revisings anyway, for otherwise his physics could not develop further. He overrides his own insistence on the homogeneity of matter in Part II in order to reinstate some heterogeneity in the domain of physics. But he does all this with a curious unawareness of his infidelity to the method. His misplaced confidence in the simplicity of starting-points, the transparency of rational relations, and the ease of extrapolation is at once a contributing factor in getting the project of modern physics started, and an unfortunate blindness to the multifarious, prodigal, irreducible complexity of nature.

THE PLENUM AND SUBTLE MATTER

Some preliminary comments about Descartes's treatment of the plenum and subtle matter will set the stage for this discussion. Descartes rejects the void in part because of his conflation of the domains of geometry and physics: space and its instantiation *res extensa* differ only as genus and instance. (The last chapter exhibited some of the difficulties generated by this conflation.) Descartes discusses a few of the consequences of his assumption of the plenum in Part II, sections 33–5, just before he expounds the laws of motion. His answer to the question, how can this assumption be reconciled with the fact of motion, resembles that of Aristotle.

It has been shown above that all places are full of bodies and that the size of each part of matter is always exactly equal to that of its place; (so that it is not possible for it to fill a bigger one or to fit into a smaller one, or for any other body to find room in its place while it is there). From this it follows that no body can move except in a (complete circle of matter or ring of bodies which all move at the same times); in such a way that it drives another body out of the place which it enters, and that other takes the place of still another, and so on until the last, which enters the place left by the first one at the moment at which the first one leaves it.[2]

82 *Laws of Motion*

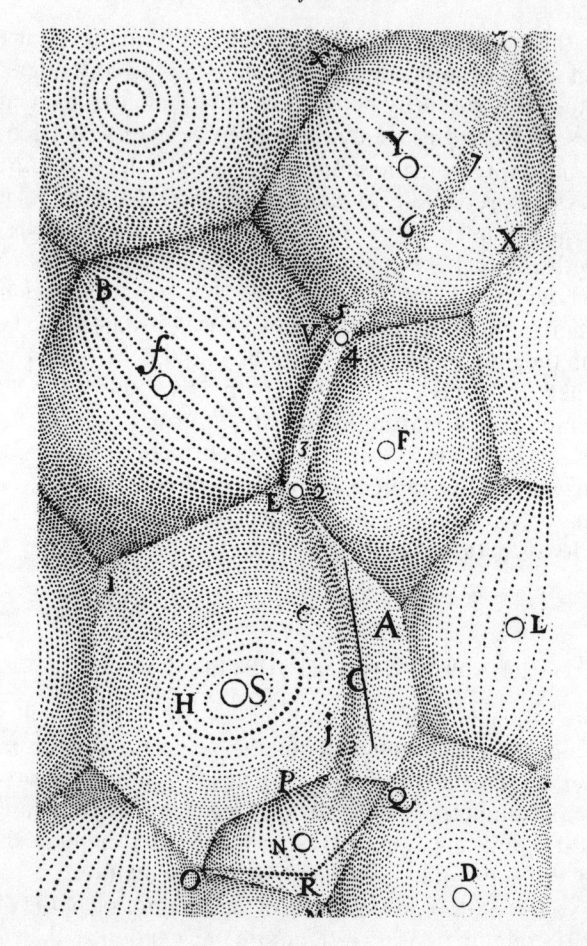

Fig. 4.1

An illustration of this situation appears later on in Part III (Fig. 4.1).[3] This provides an interesting partial solution to Descartes's quandary that liquids (as he defines them) in themselves exhibit no physical unity at the level of 'common motion'. The circuits of matter just described—vortices—constitute unities at a higher level of organization; the shared motion is curved motion, compounded pointwise out of straight line motion as particles collide and deflect each other. A vortex moreover does have, according to Descartes, a significant interdependence among parts and the whole. While some vortices may be perfectly circular, others may be irregular in shape (Fig. 4.2).

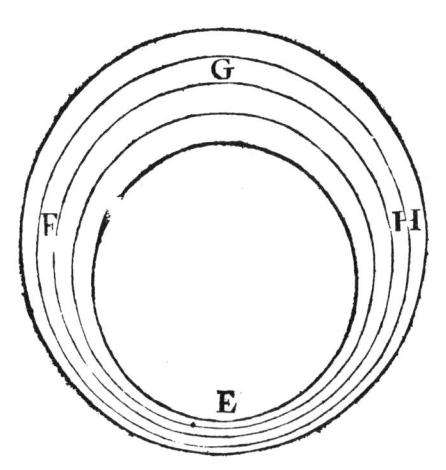

Fig. 4.2

So, without there being any condensation or vacuum, all the matter contained in the space EFGH can move in a circle. The part of it which is near E can move toward G and that which is near G can simultaneously move toward E, provided only that (since we are supposing the space at G to be four times as wide as at E, and twice as wide as at F and H) we also suppose the movements to be four times as rapid at E as at G, and twice as rapid as at F and H. Similarly, in all remaining places, we can suppose that speed of movement compensates for narrowness of space. Thus, in any given length of time, the same quantity of matter will pass through one section of the circle as through another.[4]

A change of motion of the particles at one place on the circuit requires a compensating change of motion at every other part of the circuit, and Descartes sharpens up this claim of a systematic interdependency among parts by specifying that the product of velocity times area of cross-section must be constant at every point of the circuit. The occurrence of vortices within a liquid seems to answer the question how unities can exist there without the presence of a container, and vortices seem to be interesting models of unity. (Though so far Descartes has left unspecified what happens at the boundary of a vortex, or indeed what constitutes such a boundary.)

A difficulty immediately arises, however, for vortices defined in this way. It is impossible to choose shapes for the impenetrable bits whirling around in vortical motion, so that they pack into space leaving no interstices where a void could lurk. How then can matter fill these interstices? Because of this problem, Descartes again comes up against his own finitism, as he does in the *Geometry*. There, he is tempted to regard the infinitely iterated pointwise construction of curves as completed, but then risks losing the rationale behind the articulated levels of his hierarchy. But if he admits that a curve constructed pointwise does not have full status as a curve, it may not be available as a constructing curve. Here, Descartes must accept the end-result of another infinitely iterated process, dividing a finite bit of matter into an indefinite number of pieces. The result must be perilously close to a point mass, an infinitesimal bit of matter.[5] In section 34, just following his introduction of the vortex, he writes:

It must, however, be admitted that there is in this movement something which our mind cannot (fully) understand, even though we perceive it to be true: namely, a division of certain parts of matter to infinity, or an indefinite division into so many particles that we cannot conceive of any so small that we do not understand that it is in fact divided into others even smaller. For it is not possible for the matter which now fills the space G to fill successively all the spaces of very gradually decreasing size which are between G and E,

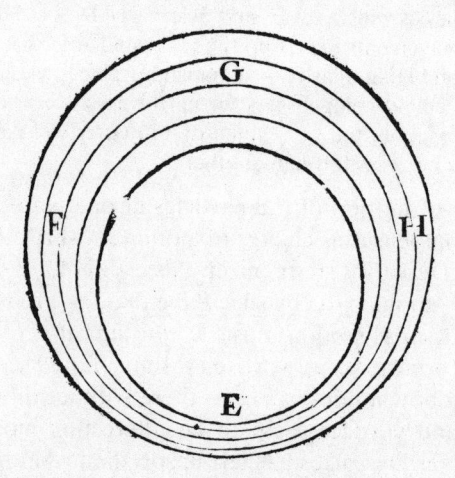

Fig. 4.3

unless some of these parts adapt their shape (and divide as necessary to fit exactly) to the innumerable dimensions of those spaces. In order for this to occur, all the particles into which one can imagine such a unit of matter to be divisible, and which are truly innumerable, must move slightly with respect to one another; and however slight this movement, it is nevertheless a true division.[6]

Thus Descartes introduces 'subtle matter', which he calls 'first element matter' in the cosmogony of Part III to which I shall return in the next section.

Subtle matter is a strange stuff which turns out to have no impenetrability because its potential divisibility has been wholly and kinematically actualized as division. It can thus perform all the functions of the void for Descartes when he needs such a stand-in. According to the metaphysics of the age, *res extensa* is supposed to be impenetrable but divisible. Two distinct spheres with the same radius, made of *res extensa*, can only exist side by side; they cannot melt into or pass through each other and must remain two entities. But two purely geometrical spheres of equal radius can be superimposed one on the other; in fact, that is a good way of demonstrating their congruence. But then there is only one entity, since the sole distinction between the two was initially their side-by-sideness and that has been abolished. Thus purely geometrically shaped volumes, while interesting unities, are not true individuals but only equivalence classes. The impenetrability of matter is an important condition for the existence of individuals which persist as one thing.

When Descartes banishes the impenetrability of subtle matter, the results are therefore metaphysically rather anomalous, for how can matter behave like void? Moreover, if it does, then the boundary conditions which force Descartes, like Aristotle, to posit circuits of matter as the only possible kind of movable configuration in a plenum are lacking. Any configuration can exist if there is enough subtle matter, acting like empty ambient space, to accommodate it. The rationale for choosing vortices as the characteristic physical complex disappears.

THE THREE LAWS OF MOTION

Such considerations prompt a closer look at Descartes's accounts of the impenetrability and divisibility of matter. For he does not just assert that *res extensa* has these qualities, but offers physical explanations of them in his laws of nature, which thus constitute a second, kinematic-dynamic and not merely geometrical system of relations. The first law of nature states 'that each thing, as far as is in its power, always remains in the same state; and that consequently, when it is once moved, it always continues to move'.[7] The second law states 'that all movement is, of itself, along straight lines'.[8] In section 43, Descartes uses these principles to account for the impenetrability of matter.

We must however notice carefully at this time in what the force of each body to act against another or to resist the action of that other consists: namely, in the single fact that each thing strives, as far as is in its power, to remain in the same state, in accordance with the first law stated above. From this it follows that a body which is joined to another has some force to resist being separated from it, while a body which is separate has some force to remain at rest, and consequently to resist everything which can change it; while a moving body has some force to continue its motion, i.e. to continue to move at the same speed and in the same direction.[9]

The parts of a body which is 'one thing' will strive to remain, with the persistence of inertial motion, in the state of common motion or common rest which constituted them as a unity in the first place. Note that since the constitution of parts as a unity in virtue of common motion or common rest is independent of the thing's shape, size or speed, so too should its impenetrability be, which is after all just the perduration of its unity. According to this definition, matter is impenetrable if it is undivided, and penetrable if it has been divided; a physical object is either 'one thing' or it is not. There are no degrees of such penetrability. Indeed, strictly speaking, if a division has taken place, then what results is not one penetrable bit of matter, but two impenetrable bits of matter. All finite bits of matter, as such, therefore exhibit impenetrability. Subtle matter has no impenetrability because its parts are infinitesimal (certainly smaller than any finite quantity) and share no common motion. It has no impenetrability because it is all divided; there no longer remains any finite bit in which impenetrability, or unity, could reside.

But this definition of impenetrability, stemming from unity as common motion, is not adequate to the demands which the second relational structure will put on the simples of physics. Descartes shifts his definition right in the middle of section 43, which concludes,

Furthermore, this force must be measured not only by the size of the body in which it is, and by the (area of the) surface which separates this body from those around it; but also the speed and nature of its movement, and by the different ways in which bodies come in contact with one another.[10]

Bodies can have more or less of this force, apparently, depending on their size, shape, and speed; this kind of impenetrability has degrees, so that bodies can be ranked as more or less divisible, when another body meets them in impact. Descartes invokes modes other than common motion or common rest to explain variable degrees of integrity in material particles, to accord with the second relational structure.

Descartes defines force as the product of 'bulk' times speed (a scalar), an invariant which I will hereafter write somewhat imprecisely as mv. God, by injecting motion into the monolith of *res extensa*, creates a quantum of force which He then maintains at a constant level at every moment of His 'continuous creation'. A diminuation of mv somewhere in the universe must be balanced somewhere by a compensating increase; this is the import of the third law of motion, akin to a conservation of momentum principle. Rational relations among colliding bits of matter are therefore defined as those which preserve the equilibrium of momenta in the universe.

40. The third law: that a body, upon coming in contact with a stronger one, loses none of its motion; but that, upon coming in contact with a weaker one, it loses as much as it transfers to that weaker body.[11]

Descartes uses his notion of force to strengthen the integrity of physical simples, which in its original formulation as common motion would quickly be overcome by impact. Sometimes Descartes means by force a body's ability to resist deflection, while it persists as one thing, and sometimes he means its ability to resist division, which would break up its unity and make it two or more things. The first interpretation of force is presupposed and illustrated in the seven rules of impact. In this case the role of impact is to regulate the world according to the principle of conservation of momentum, to make physical interaction mathematizable and predictable, and to maintain the status quo among the furniture of the universe. The very same objects which enter into collisions in the seven rules also (allegedly) emerge from them.

The second interpretation of force is presupposed and illustrated in a passage at the very end of Part II and in the cosmogony of Part III.[12] There the function of impact, though Descartes never imagines any violation of the conservation of momentum, is to change and differentiate the furniture of the universe by breaking up particles, and its outcome is indeterminate and unpredictable. Under both interpretations, the force of impenetrability admits of degrees. However, in the first case, it increases proportionately as mass (bulk) and as speed (a body at rest is an exceptional case, but in general fast objects win out over slow ones); in the second case, it increases proportionately with mass (bulk) and inversely with speed. Cartesian method calls upon the second system of rational relations both to constitute and preserve the simples of the domain of physics which must be homogeneous in a strong sense, and to differentiate them.

Descartes's seven rules of impact specify the cases of the third law of motion. In this context, force is taken to measure an object's power to resist deflection and to deflect another object, but the disruption of an object's unity is never even entertained as a possibility. Objects which are one persist as one before and after collision in each of the seven rules. Indeed, the intelligibility and determinacy of these rules, their ability to predict outcomes, depend on the prior identification of stable physical unities as the participants in these interactions. Thus construed, Descartes's rules of impact are intended to regulate and maintain the status quo of the universe, so that every bit of matter is accorded its appropriate portion of motion.

The following schematic representation will be useful for the discussion. In every case Descartes supposes that all motion before and after collision takes place on the same straight line (i.e. there is no angular deflection), that all motion is uniform and that, if motion alters in direction or magnitude because of the collision, the alteration is instantaneous.[13]

1. $m_B = m_C$, $v_B = v_C$. The bodies approach each other and collide; upon collision, both bodies rebound with their initial speeds, but reversed directions: $v_B' = v_B$ and $v_C' = v_C$. (v is a scalar.)

2. $m_B > m_C$, $v_B = v_C$. The bodies approach each other and collide; upon collision, only C rebounds, and both bodies move away together with the same speeds: $v_B' = v_B$ and $v_C' = v_C$ but with reversed direction.

3. $m_B = m_C$, $v_B > v_C$. The bodies approach each other and collide; upon collision, only C rebounds, and both bodies move away together, but at a new speed, v_B' (and v_C') $= v_C + \frac{1}{2}(v_B - v_C)$.

4. $m_C > m_B$, $v_B > 0$, $v_C = 0$. B collides with C (which does not budge) and rebounds at the same speed: $v_B' = v_B$.

5. $m_B > m_C$, $v_B > 0$, $v_C = 0$. B collides with C and they both move off together in B's initial direction with speed v_B' (and v_C') $= m_B v_B/(m_B + m_C)$.

6. $m_B = m_C$, $v_B > 0$, $v_C = 0$. B collides with C and they both rebound, with reversed directions and new speeds $v_B' = \frac{3}{4} v_B$ and $v_C' = \frac{1}{4} v_B$.

7. $m_C > m_B$, $v_B > v_C$. B and C are moving in the same directions, so that B will eventually collide with C. There are three sub-cases.

   (i) $v_B/v_C > m_C/m_B$. Upon collision, the bodies move off together in B's initial direction, both with speed v_B' $(= v_C') = (m_B v_B + m_C v_C)/m_B + m_C$.
   (ii) $v_B/v_C < m_C/m_B$. Upon collision, B rebounds in the opposite direction. $v_B' = v_B$ but oppositely directed, and $v_C' = v_C$.
   (iii) $v_B/v_C = m_C/m_B$. Upon collision, B rebounds in the opposite direction with diminished speed $v_B' = ((3m_B + m_C)/2(m_B + m_C)) v_B$, and C continues in the same direction with augmented speed $v_C' = ((2 - (3m_B + m_C))/2 (m_B + m_C)) v_C$.

These rules have been criticized on various grounds ever since Descartes wrote them. They are hardly a complete set of rules, since they only treat collisions along a line; they are not preserved under a transformation of inertial frame; they do not accord with observation; and so forth. My criticism rests rather on the fact that they are incompatible with Descartes's earlier pronouncements on the kind of integrity which physical objects have, and moreover that when taken in conjunction with certain of those pronouncements, they lead to unacceptable results.

Note that in none of the outcomes of these collisions do the bodies involved shatter. Since a physical body left to itself according to Descartes's first two laws of motion will continue in its initial state, a body which is one will persist as one unless something interferes with it. But what could that interference be? The only kind of physical interaction Descartes allows is impact. If his laws of motion are intended as a complete set, and if in none of the cases are the unities of physical bodies broken up, then the particles which God creates at the beginning of the world are *de facto* atoms.

Even worse, if we analyse these outcomes taking seriously Descartes's definition of a physical unity we find that in four of the nine cases, the 'two' objects B and C move off together at the same speed, i.e. with the same motion. Though Descartes continues to refer to them as if they were distinct, by his earlier definitions they constitute one object because they share a common motion; they are even contiguous and at rest with respect to each other. In other words, not only do collisions thus defined never result in disintegration but their general tendency is to result in aggregation, producing larger and larger objects out of the association of smaller parts in a common motion. The rules will also result in a general slowing-down of matter. In every case, the resulting speeds remain the same or are adjusted so that no speed, whether augmented or diminished, ever surpasses the maximum speed of either object entering the collision.

Thus, the long-term drift of Descartes's rules of impact will be to produce slower and larger particles. No matter how God originally broke up the monolith into bits, the physical interaction among those bits will eventually make the universe revert to the state of the monolith, one indefinitely large thing with zero velocity.

Perhaps Descartes could save the situation from the threat of the monolith if he hypothesized that God originally created the world with large tracts of subtle matter. Surely subtle matter would be immune to this process of aggregation. In fact, subtle matter is too immune to it; there can be no collisions between bits of subtle matter in conformity with the seven rules because the bulk of such bits is less than any finite amount. The conservation of momentum in every such interaction would be just $0 = 0$. To put it another way, subtle matter cannot be a carrier of Cartesian force, *mv*, for it does not allow of physical interaction within itself (if that locution makes sense) nor with finite objects. It is, as I mentioned earlier, a stand-in for the void. But that means that if there is a process by which finite objects can be converted into subtle matter, and we shall see that there is, then the conservation of momentum is threatened. Descartes's rules of impact require the prior availability of stably persisting finite objects so that they can be applicable to physical reality. And only on this condition do they yield determinate, quantifiable, and predictable outcomes.

Descartes never worries about the threat of a possible reinstatement of the monolith. The possibility never occurs to him for two reasons. One is that he appeals to geometric individuation (as he so often unwittingly does) when he characterizes the aftermaths of collisions; he always refers to the ingredient bodies as two bodies, B and C, even after they have become kinematically one. Second, he invokes impact as the mechanism for breaking up matter, never noticing that this function is incompatible with the assumptions and indeed the coherence of his rules of impact, as I show in the next section.

THE DIVISION OF MATTER

The only possibility for material interaction in Descartes's physics, and thus for the division of matter, is impact. Divisible matter is actually divided initially by God, but thereafter (with God's maintenance) by collisions. Descartes offers a description of the outcome of collisions in terms of the primary (quantifiable) properties of the ingredient objects in the cosmogony of Part III, and thus brings in the back door much stronger versions of physical unity than common motion or rest. This is his account of the origins of the three kinds of matter.

Beginning at section 45 of Part III, Descartes tells the story of the genesis of the world quoted in the last chapter: God begins with starting-points which are 'simple and easy to know', and proceeds according to the order of reasons.

Let us therefore suppose, if you please, that God, in the beginning, divided all the matter of which he formed the visible world into parts as equal as possible and of medium size, that is to say that their size was the average of all the various sizes of the parts which now compose the heavens and the stars. And let us suppose that He endowed them collectively with exactly that amount of motion which is still in the world at present.[14]

God then allows all these homogeneous (equal in size and speed) particles to start colliding with each other. The collisions start to break the particles up and to differentiate them, Descartes claims, in a manner related to the primary qualities of the particles. Small but finite spherical particles, 'second element matter', are created first; whatever shapes the particles had in the beginning,

> it was impossible for them not to become spherical with the passing of time because of their various circular motions. And because the force by which they were moved in the beginning was sufficient to separate them from one another; that same force, enduring (in them subsequently), was also undoubtedly great enough to break off all their angles as they came in contact with one another, for this effect required less force than the previous one had.[15]

On this account, spherical particles are more stable kinds of unity than particles with edges, for the latter inevitably decompose into the former, which then persist indefinitely. Thus, despite his earlier claim at Part II, section 55, that 'the parts of solid bodies are not joined to each other by any other bond than their own rest (relative to each other)',[16] Descartes invokes the mode of shape to allow a differentiation of matter in his physics and the attendant possibility of degrees of unity. The sequel to this passage, introducing 'first element matter' or subtle matter, appeals to the modes of size and speed to further differentiate *res extensa* and bestow degrees of cohesiveness on it.

The free edges, or scrapings, from the whittling process that makes spheres of angular fragments Descartes portrays as the ancestors of subtle matter, which are then worn down to become very tiny and very fast; indeed, the smaller and faster they become, the more quickly they are ground down to subtle matter. Thus here, penetrability, while inversely proportional to bulk, is directly proportional to speed.

> 50. That the particles of this more subtle matter are very easily divided. For it must be noted that the smaller these scrapings of other particles are, the more easily they can be moved and (subsequently) reduced to parts even tinier: because the smaller they are, the more surface area they have in proportion to their bulk, (and the size of this surface area causes them to meet correspondingly more bodies which attempt to move or divide them, while their small quantity of matter makes them correspondingly less able to resist their force); and they encounter bodies in proportion to their surface and are divided according to their bulk.

51. And that these particles move very rapidly. We must also notice that, although the scrapings (thus detached from the parts of matter which are becoming rounded) have no motion which does not come from these parts, they must however move much more quickly.[17]

The smaller and quicker these particles are, the more often they encounter other bodies, and thus, Descartes reasons, the more often they are divided. He gives an analogy to explain how their speed is continually augmented.

The reason is that the (larger) parts, which travel by straight and open paths, drive this scraping (or dust which is among them) through other paths which are oblique and narrower. Similarly, we see that by closing a bellows quite slowly, we force the air out of it quite rapidly, because the opening through which this air emerges is small.[18]

But this analogy is at odds with Descartes's seven rules of impact, which in no case allow a final speed higher than any entering into the interaction.

Subsequently, Descartes describes the formation of 'third element matter'. It is formed when scrapings of still finite dimension are compressed between globules of second matter and, retaining the shape of their containers, bear three grooves (Fig. 4.4).

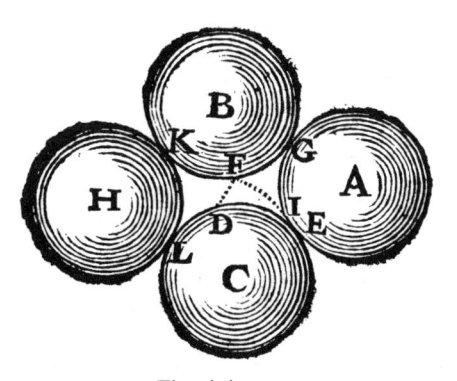

Fig. 4.4

88. That those tiny particles which have the least speed easily transfer to others that which they have, and adhere to one another. So therefore, in the matter of the first element, there are certain scrapings less divided than the rest and less rapidly agitated. And since we are supposing these scrapings to have been torn away from the angles of the particles of the second . . . it is

impossible for these scrapings not to have extremely angular shapes, ill-adapted to movement. As a result, they easily adhere to one another and transfer a great part of their agitation to those other scrapings which are the tiniest and most rapidly agitated . . .

90. What the shape of these particles, which from now on we shall call grooved, is. Of course, they must be triangular in cross-section, because they frequently pass through those narrow triangular spaces which are created when three globules of the second element touch.[19]

Third element matter is cohesive enough to stick together, but malleable enough to take on the shape of what impinges on it. Descartes explains its cohesiveness by the irregular, burr-like shapes of its component parts, and its ultimate shape by reference to the triangular containers formed by tangent spheres.

Thus Descartes introduces a threefold differentiation of *res extensa* by appealing to the modes of shape, size, and speed, and external items like shaping containers, as factors variably influencing the persistent unity of bits of matter; the appeal is inconsistent with the definition of unity as common motion. But at this point a stronger definition of unity is in fact required, for the relatively weak unity of common motion in combination with a construal of impact that allows shattering would disintegrate *res extensa* altogether. This outcome becomes clear in section 63, at the very end of Part II, where Descartes explains why a nail can be broken into two parts by a hammer, and not the human hand. The passage occurs in a discussion of the distinction between solid and liquid bodies.

We see many bodies much smaller than our hands, (the particles of) which adhere together so firmly that they cannot be divided by any force of our hands. Now, if their parts are joined by no other bond than the fact that they are contiguous and at rest, and since any body which is at rest can be set in motion by a moving body which is larger than itself; at first glance there seems to be no reason why, for example, an iron nail . . . cannot be divided into two parts solely by the force of our hands. For each half of this nail may be considered to be an individual body; and since one half is smaller than our hand, it seems that it ought to be possible to move it by the force of our hand and thus separate it from the other half.[20]

Descartes's solution to this conundrum is interesting but not immediately relevant. What is more important is his account of the divisibility of matter. First, he invokes individuation by pure geometry, shaped volume: each half of the nail can be considered one thing even before the nail is broken. And then he claims that any other body which is larger than the half-nail ought to be able to carry off the half-nail without affecting the other half left behind, since they 'are joined by no other bond than the fact that they are contiguous and at rest, and since any body which is at rest can be set in motion by a moving body which is larger than itself'.

This account of divisibility by collision, which appeals to unity in virtue of common motion (while also tacitly appealing to unity in virtue of geometric shape), produces odd results. Primarily, it entails that any collision whatsoever may result in shattering, and that any body may shatter any other body. For any finite body A, no matter how small in relation to another body B, will be larger than some finite bit of B (which by purely geometric individuation can be considered a separate thing) and can carry it off or (in case A is at rest) make it rebound. If A is bigger than B, it can carry off, or make rebound, any part of B. And *pari passu* the same holds for B in relation to A. Not only can, indeed must, all collisions result in shatterings then, but the outcome of these collisions is indeterminate and cannot be specified. Will A shatter B or will B shatter A? What bit of A or B will be sent flying? The possibilities are infinite. Thus in the absence of the availability of more strongly stable physical particles, the outcomes of collision cannot be predicted or quantified.

Cartesian method requires that a subject-matter begin with certain simples, and that complexes be constructed from them by association in rational relations. I have argued that Descartes's physics begins with bits of matter which are one in virtue of sharing a common, uniform, rectilinear motion; and sometimes he also appeals to geometric shape. But unity in virtue of common motion or geometric shape are such weak kinds of integrity that they cannot prevent the disruption of physical unities upon each occurrence of the only kind of physical interaction, collision. For in the former model of unity there is no interdependence among parts; the deflection of one part of 'one thing' has no effect whatsoever on the other parts, which continue undisturbed in their common motion or common rest, as much or as little 'one thing' as they were before. Alterations in some parts do not call for compensatory changes in other parts or in the whole. And in the latter, geometric model of unity the interdependence among parts has nothing to do with physical interaction; mathematical items are parts of other such items in very different ways from physical parts which compose wholes.

Thus, unless Descartes does something to shore up the unity of his simples, the Cartesian universe must disintegrate to subtle matter in short order. That is, he must appeal to modes and external factors which he told us at the beginning could not be relevant to the unity of a physical object. In other words, he must change the definition of what it is to be one thing in physics, the definition of a simple, in order to save his physics; but in so doing he violates the requirements of his method.

This part of my discussion began as an examination of impenetrability according to Descartes: what it is about matter that lets it exclude other matter, push other matter, and resist being pushed by it. In light of this discussion, the anomaly of subtle matter becomes apparent. For while subtle matter has no force, in the sense of being able to resist finite particles which move through it without collisions, as if it were empty space, it is impenetrable in the sense that it excludes other matter. In a volume full of subtle matter, there is no room for anything else. Descartes claims that all matter is homogeneous and, among other things, of constant density, no matter how the variable injections of motion (consequent on the action of God or collisions) break it up. If the whole world were composed of subtle matter, it would be a plenum of subtle matter and nothing else would 'fit' into it. There would not be room for a fish or a knife or a mote, and that is surely a kind of impenetrability. Moreover it would have no parts in Descartes's sense of a part, and thus would exhibit only the unarticulated unity of partlessness. A world of subtle matter is after all hard to distinguish from the totality of inert *res extensa*. And Descartes's reductive method fails to establish a plausible integrity for mid-range physical objects, between the infinitesimal dust of subtle matter and the indefinitely extended monolith of inert *res extensa*.

Descartes's explanation of how applied mathematics is possible is that *res extensa* differs from Euclidean space only as the individual from the genus, by a mere difference of concept: they share the same relational structure. In this chapter, I have argued that a tacit change of the relational structure forces a change in the items of physics, making them less plausibly identical with the items of geometry. In the next chapter, I will show why, despite Descartes's conflation of the subject-matters of geometry and physics, his mathematization of physics seems in retrospect so limited. His impoverishment of geometry, excluding or relegating to the side-

Laws of Motion

lines areas and volumes, curves and infinitesimals, transcendental numbers and curves, removes many elements that prove central to the mathematization of physics in the hands of Galileo, Torricelli, Leibniz, and Newton. It ironically puts his geometry at odds with the physical articulation he posits for *res extensa*. And the demands of his method also tend to set aside dynamic and temporal considerations in the development of his physics.

Notes

1. For an interesting treatment of the classical texts and their early modern reception, see S. Drake and I. E. Drabkin (eds.) *Mechanics in Sixteenth Century Italy* (Madison: University of Wisconsin Press, 1969), esp. the introductory essay by S. Drake (3–60) and the bibliography (391–420). F. De Gandt also takes up this set of issues in his 'L'Analyse de la percussion chez Galilée et Torricelli' in *L'Œuvre de Torricelli*, ed. F. De Gandt (Nice: Publications de la Faculté de Nice et Sciences Humaines de Nice, 1989), 53–77; and in his Doctorat d'État, *Force et Géométrie: La théorie Newtonienne de la force centripète, présenté dans son contexte* (Paris, 1987).
2. *Principia Philosophiae*, pp. 55–6; 58–9.
3. Ibid. 294 (Plate vi); 88.
4. Ibid. 55–6; 58–9. Illus. 289 (Plate I); 59.
5. In his 'The Infinite in Descartes' Conversation with Burman', *Archiv für Geschichte der Philosophie*, 69 (1987), 140–63, esp. 148–9, R. Ariew argues that Descartes consistently equates the indefinite with the potential infinite, so strictly that it can never be assimilated to the actual infinite. While I agree with Ariew's claim that, metaphysically, Descartes requires such a strict distinction, I would hold that in this case he is pushed by the requirements of his physics to postulate the 'unthinkable', that matter might be actually divided to infinity.
6. *Principia Philosophiae*, pp. 56–7; 59–60.
7. Ibid. 59; 62–3.
8. Ibid. 60–1; 63–5.
9. Ibid. 63; 66–7.
10. Ibid.
11. Ibid. 61–2; 65.
12. Ibid. 75–6; 77–8 and 106 f; 100 f.
13. Ibid. 64–9; 68–70.
14. Ibid. 106–7; 100–1.
15. Ibid. 108; 103–4.
16. Ibid. 70; 71.
17. Ibid. 109–10; 104–5.
18. Ibid.
19. Ibid. 133–4; 144–6. Illus. 299 (Plate x); 146.
20. Ibid. 75–6; 77–8.

5
Historical Context of Cartesian Physics

GENERATIONS of scholars have noticed that Descartes's claim to mathematize physics was a philosophical promise that he was unable to keep in a thoroughgoing and effective way. This lapse is curious; it has prompted much discussion, and various attempts to characterize and explain Descartes's work at the intersection of geometry and mechanics. Paul Tannery, in a footnote to Descartes's interesting letter on Galileo's *Dialogues* (to Mersenne, 11 October 1638), observes:

> He is content to deny the assumptions on which Galileo based his dynamics, because henceforth, according to Descartes, he would understand motion only in a medium, and refuse to admit that physically unrealizable abstractions could aid the progress of science. He lacked a sense for the conditions under which mathematics applies to problems (other than those concerned with numbers, formulae and geometric magnitudes), a sense which Galileo by contrast possessed in the highest degree.[1]

Alexandre Koyré makes a similar argument in one of his *Études Galiléennes*, viewing Descartes's methodological decision to follow the order of reasons as the cause of his inability to integrate mathematics and physics more fully. Descartes's decision in the early 1630s to order whole subject matters according to the analytic order of reasons, Koyré maintains, accounts for why he 'lost all the concrete gains of the "new science", of that physico-mathematics which had been unfolding under his eyes [in the 1620s], to whose creation he himself had so forcefully contributed.'[2] Even Jules Vuillemin, while arguing that Descartes's method understood as the construction of extended proportions organizes his mathematics and metaphysics, must admit nevertheless that his treatment of two important curves, the logarithmic curve and the logarithmic spiral, is barred from finding physical application by assumptions traceable to his methodology.[3]

In this chapter, I will explain in some detail why Descartes's success in combining mathematics and physics is so limited, on the basis of my conclusions in the foregoing chapters. My explanation naturally runs parallel to that of Koyré, for I hold that the way in which Cartesian method impoverishes as well as organizes the fields to which it is applied renders geometry as inapt for physics as it leaves physics unready for important new developments in mathematics. It would be unfair to limit my argument to the *Geometry* and the *Principles* alone, since much of Descartes's quantified mechanics is given in his correspondence; but the testimony of the letters only reconfirms, in somewhat sharper focus, my conclusion that his reductive method is a two-edged instrument of thought, deployed with mixed results.

According to Descartes's pronouncements throughout Part II of the *Principles,* a physical object is precisely and merely an instantiation of a region of three-dimensional Euclidean space, and he reiterates this identification quite strongly in the last section of Part II of the *Principles:* 'That I do not accept or desire in Physics any other principles than in Geometry or abstract Mathematics; because all the phenomena of nature are explained thereby, and certain demonstrations concerning them can be given. . . . For I openly acknowledge that I know no kind of material substance other than that which can be divided, shaped, and moved in every possible way, and which Geometers call quantity and take as the object of their demonstrations.'[4] Thus matter, according to Descartes, has no attributes besides the quantifiable ones that stem from its extendedness. The essence of matter is then also mathematical; matter has an inherent structure articulable as Euclidean geometry. And since Descartes's great mathematical work, the *Geometry*, is designed to reformulate and rationalize classical geometry, his project of mathematizing nature would seem here to find its appropriate grounding.

However, as I argued in Chapters 1 and 2, Descartes's choice of simple and homogeneous starting-points for his geometry also excludes certain other items from serving as terms in his proportions: areas and volumes, and curves and infinitesimals. These items are central to the mathematization of physics in the hands of Galileo, Torricelli, Leibniz, and Newton. Nor does Descartes see in a clearly focused way the power of his own innovation in the *Geometry*, which allows the investigation of curves as algebraic-geometrical-numerical hybrids, a multivalence that is the key to their investigation and their employment in physics in the latter half of the seventeenth century. For Descartes, curves are primarily constructing curves, to be used to construct points in the solution of

Historical Context of Cartesian Physics 101

problems, and hence he never recognizes their rich multivalence and variety. The mathematics of Descartes's *Geometry*, pruned and homogenized as it is by the demands of method, is then curiously unsuited for the representations required by contemporary physics. In Chapters 3 and 4, we examined some of the difficulties that stem from Descartes's identification of the subject-matter of geometry and that of physics. Either his simples do not have sufficient integrity to serve as the objects of physics, or he must introduce a divergence between the objects of geometry and the objects of physics which the demands of his method will not allow him to recognize as such. In this chapter we will see that his method strips the objects of physics of their temporality and dynamism as well. The conflation of domains stands in the way of their further integration; it assumes as completely accomplished a unification that can only be partial and indeed still remains to be carried out. The clearest way to make my point here is to contrast Descartes's approach to problems also of interest to other scientists of the period, foremost among them Galileo.

THE QUANTIFICATION OF FREE FALL

Galileo's treatment of free fall in the Third Day of his *Discorsi* requires diagrams that could have no counterpart in Descartes's *Geometry* (Fig. 5.1). Theorem I, Proposition I, states: 'The time in which any space is traversed by a body starting from rest and uniformly accelerated is equal to the time in which that same space would be traversed by the same body moving at a uniform speed just before acceleration began.'[5] This is his version of the mean speed theorem. As Koyré points out, the genius of this diagram is that AB represents not the distance traversed (that role is played by the separate line CD) but the time elapsed. Galileo has wrested geometry from the geometer's preoccupation with extension, and put it in the service of the essentially temporal processes of physics.[6]

What I want to stress about the diagram is that it involves areas and a process like integration with respect to time; the parallels of the triangle AEB perpendicular to AB represent velocities, and the area of the triangle as a whole, taken to be a summation of instantaneous velocities, therefore represents distance traversed. In other words, in this diagram distance is represented in two different ways, as the line segment CD and as the area of triangle

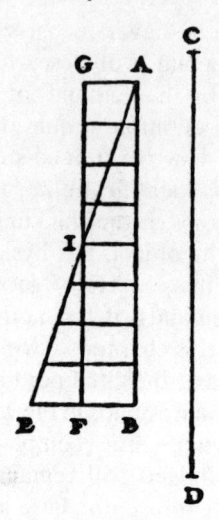

Fig. 5.1

AEB; because the second representation is a two-dimensional figure, it can exhibit how uniformly increasing velocity and time are related in the determination of a distance. Moreover, the triangle AEB is a summation of infinitesimal *momenti*, and is able to be so in virtue of the painstaking discussion of the possibility of continuously and uniformly accelerated motion that begins the Third Day. Koyré observes that Descartes the physicist rejects Galileo's arguments about the continuity of motion[7]; I want to point out that Descartes the mathematician has short-circuited the possibility that diagrams such as Galileo's have a place even in geometry.

So too with the diagram to Theorem II, Proposition II, which relates the one just discussed to the problem of free fall. The theorem states: 'The spaces described by a body falling from rest with uniformly accelerated motion are to each other as the squares of the time-intervals employed in traversing these distances.'[8] Once again there are two components to the diagram (Fig. 5.2). The line HI stands for the spatial trajectory of the falling body, but it is articulated into a sort of ruler, where the intervals representing distances traversed during equal stretches of time, HL, LM, MN etc., are marked off, forming the sequence of odd numbers, 1, 3, 5, 7 . . . as Corollary I notes. AB represents time (divided into equal intervals AD, DE, EF, etc.) with perpendicular instantaneous

Historical Context of Cartesian Physics 103

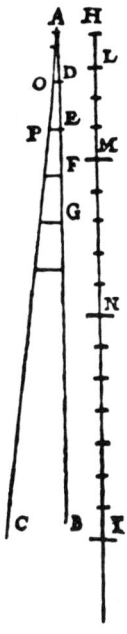

Fig. 5.2

velocities raised upon it, generating a series of areas. Distance traversed again has two distinct representations; this time one is geometric and the other numerical. The distinction is as important as the correspondence in the investigations of mechanics and mathematics leading from Galileo to the calculus at the end of the century, particularly in the reasoning that gave Leibniz his central insight into the calculus.[9] But Descartes's conflation of number and geometry stands in the way of such thinking. Nowhere in the *Geometry* does Descartes discuss how to coordinate the combinatorial patterns of number theory and geometrical results.

As it happens, Descartes in his youth (in 1619 and again in 1629) considered the problem of free fall. Beeckman proposed a version of it to him, and in his private journal, he sketched out a solution to it (Fig. 5.3).[10] Descartes takes the line ADB to represent, not the time elapsed but the distance traversed. Since he considers the lines perpendicular to AB as representing speed, triangle ADE stands for the 'quantity of motion' as the body traverses AD, and the quadrilateral DECB the 'quantity of motion' as the body traverses

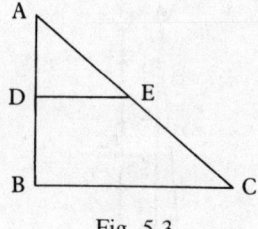

Fig. 5.3

DB. Since the latter is three times the former, he concludes that the body moves through the second interval of distance three times as quickly, and thus that in free fall, speed increases proportionally to the distance traversed, not to time.

Ten years later in 1629, Descartes sent Mersenne another version of his solution which preserves many of the same features of the earlier solution (Fig. 5.4).[11] Once again, Descartes takes the line ABC to represent extension, the trajectory of the body's fall, not time. 'In a vacuum, whatever has once begun to move will go on moving continually with a constant speed. Suppose then that there is a body at A pushed towards C by its weight. . . . The first line indicates the force of the speed impressed at the first moment; the second line, the force impressed at the second moment; and the third, the force added at the third, and so forth.'[12]

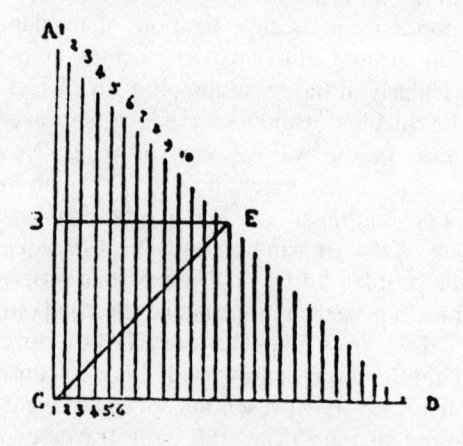

Fig. 5.4

The line CD therefore represents time marked off in instants; the triangle ABE represents 'the increase of the speed of motion' as the body proceeds from A to B, and the trapezoid BEDC the same augmentation as the body proceeds from B to C. Noting that the area of trapezoid BEDC is evidently three times the area of triangle ABE, Descartes infers that the body falls three times as quickly from B to C as from A to B, and once more erroneously concludes that in free fall the velocity increases as a function of the distance traversed, not the time. This was a common mistake in the late sixteenth and early seventeenth century; but Descartes' repetition of the error and his continuing criticisms of Galileo show that he never learned to see the crucial difference between taking time rather than space as the important parameter.

All the same, Descartes's way of reasoning about his diagram seems suggestively Italian at this early stage. Despite the archaic way of conceptualizing the physical situation in terms of impetus theory (weight is thought of as an internal force that pushes the body from A to C), he appears to be using infinitesimalistic reasoning and something like integration, to arrive at the comparison of the areas ABE and BEDC. And he supposes that the motion takes place in the void. These 'Italian' features disappear in his later attempts to model mathematically analogous kinds of physical phenomena.

For example, in his letter to Mersenne of 30 April 1639, Descartes draws a diagram superficially like the one just discussed in order to show why four times the force is required to make a string sound an octave higher (Fig. 5.5).[13] String ABC is supposed to be under twice as much tension as string EFG, even though their displacements are equal (FH = BD), and it emits a tone an octave higher than the latter. Since string ABC is under twice as much tension as EFG, Descartes claims, it will return from its displacement in half the time it takes EFG to do the same, since the inequality in the forces, given

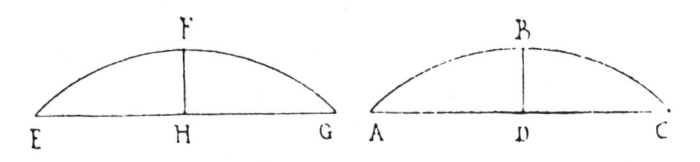

Fig. 5.5

the equality of the displacement, can only be compensated by a proportional inequality in the times.[14]

Descartes then draws a triangle KNP, where 'time can be represented by a line like KL or KN, and force by another like NO or LM or NP' (Fig. 5.6).[15] He lets the line KL represent the time in which ABC moves, and line KN the time, twice as long, in which EFG moves. The line segment NO represents the force that moves EFG over the period in which it moves; LM represents the force that moves ABC over the period (half as long) in which it moves; and NP represents the force that would move ABC over a period equal to that in which EFG moves. The triangles KLM and KNO then stand for the invariant (force × time) in the cases of the strings ABC and EFG, and therefore must be equal; so the line NP must be four times as long as NO.

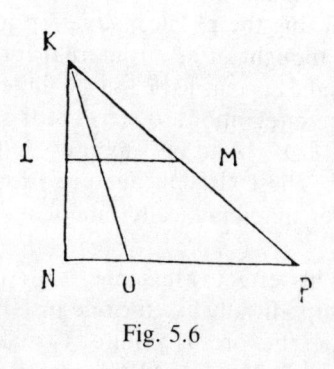

Fig. 5.6

Then Descartes makes a startling conclusion: 'The force that moves ABC must also be four times that which moves EFG; because since they are considered in themselves and without respect to any period of time, they have the same relationship to each other as when they are considered with respect to an equal time.'[16] In other words, the proper way to consider these forces is abstracted altogether from the times in which they act; so abstracted, the former force is four times the latter, NP = 4(NO). Though time is represented by the line KN, Descartes annuls the diagram's temporality by his final interpretation of it. Moreover, the physical significance of this diagram is essentially limited to relations among line segments. The final conclusion is a determination of the ratio between NO and NP. The triangles KLM and KNO clearly play an important role in the reasoning, but only as representatives of the product of line segments, not as areas resulting from a process of integration.

As this example illustrates, Descartes's choice of simples for geometry interferes with his attempts to mathematize physics. But so does his choice of simples for physics. The starting-points for the *Principles of Philosophy* are, as we have seen, bits of matter in uniform, rectilinear motion. And the sole interaction between these bits is collision, a process that changes speeds instantaneously and conserves the invariant (bulk × speed). The match between these items and processes, and the subject-matter of the *Geometry* is not after all so easy to discern.

For example, the shaped volumes that are supposed to serve as the geometrical genera for specific bits of matter have no explicit place in the *Geometry*, which is concerned primarily with straight line segments and secondarily with plane curves. And even if Descartes's geometry did contain such items, I have shown in Chapters 3 and 4 that there are deep problems concerning the coherence of associated bits of matter throughout Part II of the *Principles*. Geometrical shape, even when taken together with common motion, is insufficient as a principle of unity for physical objects.

By contrast, the straight line segments of the *Geometry* seem to correspond nicely to the inherently uniform, rectilinear trajectories of the bits of matter which are the simples of Descartes's physics, and which characterize their motion before and after impact. His model of impact, however, does not provide any really interesting geometrical context for the line *qua* trajectory; it is not the side of a triangle, the diagonal of a parallelogram, or the ordinate of a curve. Just the straight line itself, along which two material particles bump into each other, does not bring any further mathematics into play, which might illuminate the physical situation. So far, the links between Descartes's geometry and physics seem to be missing or trivial. And yet, having stipulated that all material particles are shaped volumes and that all interaction is collision and thus analysable in terms of the invariant (bulk × speed) specified in the seven rules, Descartes might have been satisfied that in principle the work of mathematizing physics was complete.[17]

What about the curves that figure in the *Geometry*? Descartes discusses curves in the *Principles* only as the trajectories of bits of matter stemming not from the nature of matter or motion, but from external exigencies imposed by the plenum: motion in a plenum can only take place, if at all, in a circuit. And the boundary condition imposed by the existence of the plenum is not strong enough to determine what precisely the curve might be, so that then the peculiar geometrical properties of that curve might be exploited in the service of physics, as Newton exploits the properties of the ellipse in Proposition XI, Book I of the *Principia*, where he derives the inverse square law.[18]

Moreover, Descartes's inability to focus on curves as algebraic-geometric-numerical hybrids contributes to his inability to regard curves as representative of the relations among continuously varying parameters. Nothing in Descartes's *Principles* is comparable to Galileo's famous analysis of projectile motion,[19] which takes the parabolic curve of a projectile's trajectory to express relations among time, distance, velocity, and the acceleration of gravity (Fig. 5.7). Nor is there anything like Newton's Proposition XI,[20] where the elliptical trajectory of a point mass circling a centre of force does much the same (Fig. 5.8). The most significant employment of curves in early modern physics does not occur to Descartes. And of course some of the most important such curves were transcendental, curves which he had excluded from mathematics altogether.

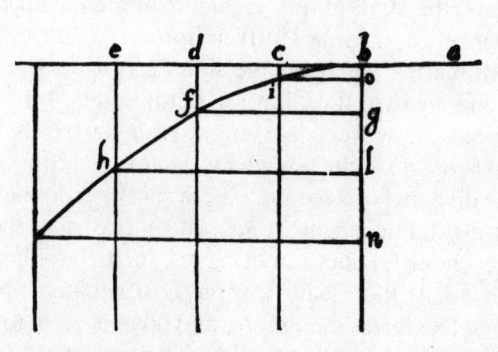

Fig. 5.7

Descartes's organization of physics short-circuits the investigation of accelerated linear and curvilinear motion. The problems concerning continuously varying forces which pose such thorny and fruitful problems for his contemporaries and successors are simply avoided. Significantly, Descartes's most mathematically

Historical Context of Cartesian Physics 109

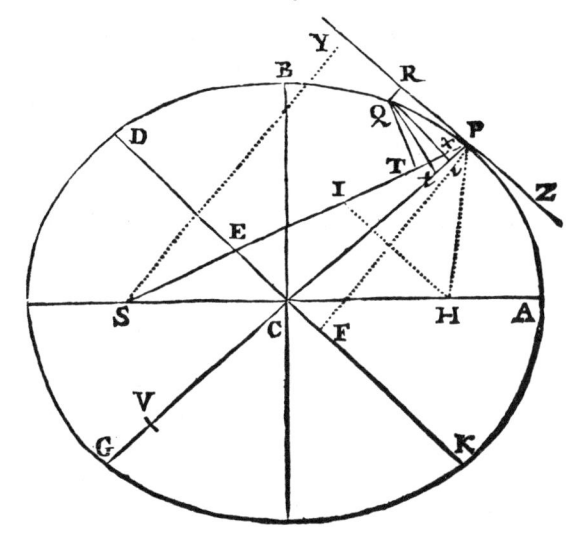

Fig. 5.8

sophisticated attempt to quantify physics occurs in a context where the temporal and dynamic dimensions of the subject-matter are irrelevant: optics is very close to a pure physical geometry, with light rays playing the roles of lines. In a sense then Descartes never makes the transition from kinematics to dynamics, as his contemporaries Galileo and Torricelli succeed in doing.

For Descartes no physical parameter, including of course what he calls 'force', varies in any essential or interesting way with time, and strictly speaking bodies never accelerate, since collisions at the microscopic level effect instantaneous changes of uniform speed. The account of the acceleration due to gravity near the surface of the earth that his vortex theory provides for macroscopic phenomena is too complicated to be quantifiable, as Descartes himself admits. And it is indeed on the grounds of this unavoidable complexity, the complexity of the articulated plenum, that Descartes gives up his attempts to quantify free fall, and rejects Galileo's mathematical model of it altogether.[21]

SIMPLE MACHINES

A possible objection to my argument so far is that it is unfair to criticize Descartes solely on the basis of the mathematization carried out in the *Principles*. For some of Descartes's mathematical physics is to be found in his letters, where he treats mechanical problems which he cannot yet link up with the a priori foundations he provides in the *Principles*. In his essay 'Descartes' Physics and Descartes' Mechanics: Chicken and Egg?',[22] Alan Gabbey argues that Descartes recognized a distinction between natural philosophy and mechanics inherited from the classical and medieval traditions. Natural philosophy was a more philosophical, systematic account of nature in itself, while mechanics was a branch of mathematics dealing with artifices and artefacts. Thus Descartes relegated much of his speculation about machines to his correspondence, in the hope perhaps that one day he or his inheritors would see how to subordinate the macroscopic, inexact phenomena of mechanics to the microscopic, exact world-view laid out in the *Principles*.

But even in his letters on mechanical topics, topics which the *Principles* passes over in silence, Descartes reveals the limitations which his method, and his mathematics shaped and restricted by method, impose on the project of quantifying physics. Two letters from the late 1630s (to Huygens, 5 October 1637 and to Mersenne, 13 July 1638)[23] contain short treatises on the simple machines (pulley, inclined plane, wedge, windlass, vice and screw, and lever). As Gabbey points out, Descartes enunciates in these two brief accounts the principle of virtual work, one of the fundamental principles of mechanics: 'The invention of all these machines is founded on a single principle, which is that the same force that can lift a weight of, for example, a hundred pounds to the height of two feet, can also lift a two hundred pound weight to the height of one foot, or a four hundred pound weight to the height of half a foot, and so forth, so long as it is applied. And this principle can't fail to be accepted, if we consider that the effect must always be proportional to the action necessary to produce it.'[24]

But by conceptualizing the simple machines in this way, in terms of the invariant (weight × distance), Descartes has effectively eliminated any discussion of how the parameter of time might enter into the action of machines. Galileo, by contrast, chooses the invariant (weight × velocity), *momento*, in his Paduan *Mechanics*, thus incorporating the dimension of time into his analytic tools.[25] The great importance of this choice of invariant has not gone unremarked by scholars. François De Gandt writes: 'This invariant [weight × velocity] permits a fertile and very flexible analysis in a

Historical Context of Cartesian Physics   111

variety of cases . . . Galileo saw quite clearly the plasticity and fecundity of the notion which he had defined and which he would call *momento*, and he made it the instrument of a series of successive extensions of the science of mechanics.'[26] The notion of *momento* proved to be especially useful in Galileo's analysis of accelerated motion, and, as taken over by Torricelli, in the analysis of percussion.

In a letter to Mersenne of 12 September 1638,[27] Descartes defends his choice of invariant, rejecting categorically the Galilean alternative. Defending his own account of the simple machines, he says that others may misunderstand it for three reasons, the first and most serious of which is, 'that many are accustomed to confound the consideration of space with that of time or speed . . . which is a fault as harmful as it is difficult to recognize.'[28] His explanation of why this opinion is mistaken is that it violates the order of reasons; for Descartes, extension must take priority over all other physical parameters. 'Because it is impossible to say anything worth while and solid about speed, without having truly explained what weight is, and together with it, all the system of the world.'[29] And he reiterates his conviction in the letter to Mersenne of 11 October 1638, apropos Roberval's *Treatise of Mechanics*: 'For he makes a conclusion of that which I make a principle, and he speaks of time or speed, where I speak of space; which is a very great error, as I have explained earlier.'[30]

Cartesian method makes the fatal elimination of temporality into a methodological requirement. And thus Koyré describes the effect this has on Descartes's physics:

Cartesian motion, this motion which is the clearest and easiest thing to know, is not, Descartes tells us, the motion of philosophers. But neither is it the motion of physicists, nor of corporeal bodies. It's the motion of geometers and of geometric entities: the motion of a point which traces a straight line, of a straight line which traces a circle . . . But these motions, contrary to physical motions, don't have any speed and don't take place in time.[31]

Descartes's preoccupation with extension to the detriment of temporality is an effect of his allegiance to the order of reasons prescribed by his method.

Descartes's reductive method focuses his mathematics on relations among finite, straight line segments, thus deflecting interest from algebraic (and transcendental) curves considered as geometric-algebraic-numerical hybrids, and from infinitesimalistic reasoning. To conclude this chapter, I would like to summarize the effect that these restrictions have on the diagrams in the *Principles*, as well as in Descartes's correspondence.

In the *Principles*, none of the diagrams involves any interesting curves that are both physically significant and mathematically articulated. The spheres and concentric circles that show up in many of them are mathematically inert and isolated; they have none of the suggestive algebraic structure that Descartes might have conferred on them if he had been interested in curves (or surfaces) as hybrids. Furthermore, since the vortex hypothesis does not specify the geometrical shape of planetary circuits, the choice of circles as representations of trajectories is arbitrary and so disconnected from the mechanical context. The spherical shape of the Cartesian corpuscles, second element matter, is likewise arbitrary and unmotivated by his physical theory. There is simply no area of overlap, accompanied by appropriately bivalent diagrams, on which Descartes's mathematics and physics can meet and mingle.

Perusal of Descartes's correspondence yields no less disappointing results. A characteristic example of his treatment of curves occurs in a letter to Mersenne dated 15 May 1634.[32] Descartes criticizes Galileo's representation of projectile motion as a parabola, and sketches two versions of his own understanding of the trajectory of a projectile (Fig. 5.9). In the case of the first trajectory where a ball is thrown up at a small angle to the zenith, Descartes merely says that the line of flight will be first curved (from A to B) and then straight (from C to D), for the upward impetus from the hand will be

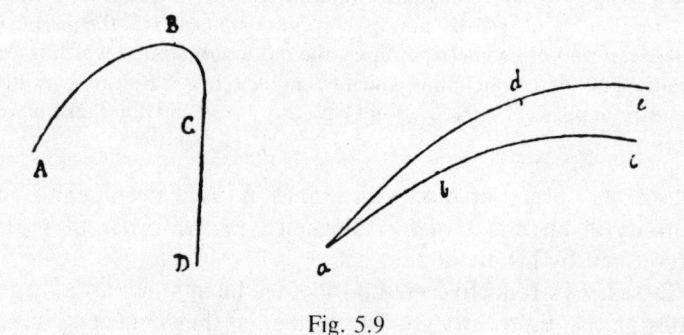

Fig. 5.9

Historical Context of Cartesian Physics 113

exhausted around B. If one throws a ball upward but more horizontally, as in the case of the second trajectory, Descartes claims that the impetus from the hand will continue until the end of the motion. 'A ball thrown from a to c and from a to e indeed describes two lines abc and ade which are of the same genus, but not for that reason similar and of the same species, and I have not yet examined what lines they might be.'[33] In neither case does Descartes attempt to characterize the curves, geometrically or algebraically. Indeed, in later letters to Mersenne (for example, 11 October 1638 and 11 March 1640 [34]) Descartes rejects Galileo's mathematical description of free fall and projectile motion in virtue of complications due to the ineluctable presence of the plenum, which appear to put a mathematically precise description beyond reach.

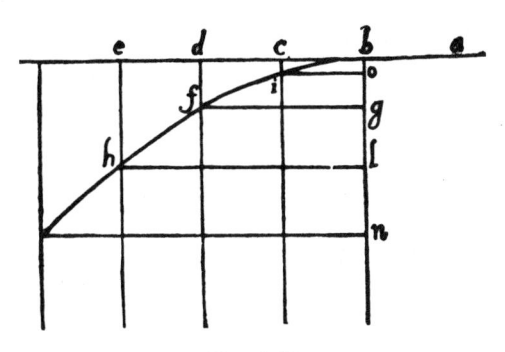

Fig. 5.10

Galileo's diagram (Fig. 5.10) of projectile motion in the *Fourth Day*[35] bears an important resemblance to Newton's famous treatment of Kepler's Law of Areas in Proposition I, Book I of the *Principia* (Fig. 5.11).[36] Both diagrams are ambiguous; they must be read at once as a collection of finite lines and areas, where the perimeter (hfib in the case of Galileo's diagram, ABCDEF in Newton's) is composed of rectilinear line segments, and also as a collection of infinitesimal as well as finite lines and areas, where the perimeter is a curve. The first reading allows the application of Euclidean theorems to the problem. The second makes the diagrams relevant to continuously accelerated motion and the action of forces. Both diagrams represent reasonings about proportions involving areas and curves, and infinitesimal lines and areas,

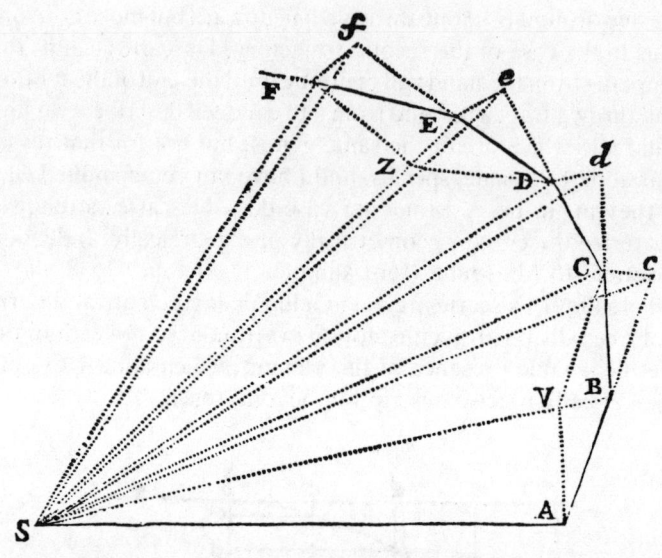

Fig. 5.11

reasonings which Descartes's methodological reordering of geometry excludes.

In their diagrams, Galileo and Newton can combine the resources of geometry and mechanics in the demonstration of fundamental results; but there are no comparable diagrams in the writings of Descartes. This is especially to be regretted, since Descartes on other occasions was quite capable of building a creative ambiguity into his mathematical schemas, as in the case of the diagram of Pappus' problem, which can read not only as a geometric locus, but also as an algebraic equation in two unknowns.

The point of this chapter is to show how the reductive instrument of Cartesian method not only opens up new avenues for mathematics and science, but also forecloses on certain possibilities already recognized by some of Descartes's contemporaries, most significantly Galileo. Reduction, by leading complexities back to simple structures, can be a powerful conduit to discovery. But its tendency to forget its own forgetting of complexity, and to conflate domains that may need to be distinguished for important reasons, adds an element of risk and uncertainty to its application. And thus it sometimes misled even so great a thinker as Descartes, who ironically embraced it as the warrant and guarantee of certainty.

Notes

1. AM iii. 77–94; Tannery's footnote is on p. 83.
2. A. Koyré, *La loi de la chute des corps: Descartes et Galilée, Études Galiléennes*, ii. (Paris: Hermann, 1939), 46.
3. Vuillemin, *Mathématiques et métaphysique chez Descartes*, pp. 11–35 and 35–51.
4. *Principia Philosophiae*, pp. 76–7; 78–9.
5. Galileo, *Dialogues Concerning Two New Sciences*, pp. 173–4. For a good discussion of Galileo's mathematical treatment of motion in relation to his medieval antecedents, see A. G. Molland, 'The Atomisation of Motion: A Facet of the Scientific Revolution', *Studies in the History and Philosophy of Science*, 13 (1982), 31–54.
6. Koyré, *La loi de la chute des corps*, ii. 67–73.
7. Ibid. 62–3.
8. Galileo, *Dialogues*, pp. 174–6.
9. See my 'Leibniz' Unification of Geometry with Algebra and Dynamics'.
10. *Cogitationes Privatae*, AT x. 219–20.
11. AM i. 83–8.
12. Ibid. i. 84–5.
13. Ibid. iii. 204–12.
14. Ibid. iii. 208.
15. Ibid. iii. 209.
16. Ibid.
17. Descartes was, however, aware that his mathematization of the microscopic realm remained to be set in relation with that of the macroscopic realm, specifically the theory of simple machines. See next section.
18. Newton, *Principia*, ed. A. Motte and F. Cajori (2 vols.; Berkeley: University of California Press, 1934), i. 56–7.
19. Galileo, *Dialogues*, pp. 248–50.
20. Newton, *Principia*, i. 56–7.
21. The aim of reductive methods is to get a cognitive, problem-solving handle on complex phenomena. But one way of acknowledging the 'irreducible' complexity of the objects of our experience is to see that there are many non-equivalent strategies of reduction, and that each has its own limitations and blind spots. In this case, Descartes's reductive procedure generates unmanageable complexity on another level.
22. Forthcoming. For related arguments, see his 'Force and Inertia in the Seventeenth Century: Descartes and Newton' in Gaukroger, *Descartes: Philosophy, Mathematics and Physics*, pp. 230–320.

23. AM ii. 31–41 and 329–46.
24. Ibid. 33.
25. *Le Meccaniche*, Galileo, *Le Opere di Galileo Galilei*, ii. 157–9.
26. 'Les *Méchaniques* attribuées à Aristote et le renouveau de la science des machines au 16ᵉ siècle', Actes du colloque, 'L'Aristotélisme au 16ᵉ siècle' in *Les Études Philosophiques*, 33 (1986), 391–405; my translation.
27. AM iii. 56–63.
28. Ibid. iii. 57.
29. Ibid. iii. 58.
30. Ibid. 77–94; the passage is on p. 86.
31. Koyré, *La loi de la chute des corps*, p. 49.
32. AM i. 256–61.
33. Ibid. i. 260.
34. Ibid. iii. 77–94 and iv. 35–42.
35. Galileo, *Dialogues*, p. 249.
36. Newton, *Principia*, i. 40.

6
Descartes's Physiology

WHILE Descartes is content with his a priori derivation of the first principles of physics from the metaphysical assumptions laid out in the *Meditations*, he admits that his investigation of particular kinds of mechanisms involves hypothetical reasoning and an empirical appeal to the senses. A measure of uncertainty, or at least a descent from metaphysical to merely moral certainty, enters the picture in the latter half of Part III and in Part IV of the *Principles* when he goes about positing, for example, microscopic mechanisms to explain specific types of astronomical and terrestrial (geological, meteorological, and chemical) phenomena.[1] Some scholars have taken this to indicate that Descartes here abandons or radically revises his conception of method.

This opinion stems, I think, from the current tendency to identify Cartesian method with the method of doubt, held to transmit perfect certainty from one proposition to another, that launches the *Meditations*. My characterization of his method throughout this book, however, has been offered in a broader, less logicizing vein. I have described it as intuitionist and reductive, so that Descartes's project is to construct objects of knowledge as ordered domains of increasingly complex objects that can be led back to inaugurating simples. While the *Meditations* have the peculiar task of grounding method in the activity of thought when it is concerned only with its own activity, the *Principles* can construct a view of the physical world on the basis of clear and distinct ideas warranted by a good and omnipotent God, and of perceptual evidence which we can be sure carries with it at least moral certainty. The task of the scientist, as Descartes sees it, is to construct mechanical models that follow from the high-level assumptions of physics and explain particular phenomena (like magnetism, combustion, or the tides) in accordance with empirical evidence.

In the previous five chapters, I have tried to show that the reductionist, monistic drift of the method creates difficulties for Descartes as he goes about setting up his geometry and his physics. It is hard for him to erect hierarchies of complexes; fidelity to method makes them collapse back to the simples, and plausible articulation of hierarchy requires importing extra structure in ways not licensed by the method. His method also tends to reductively conflate subject-matters; the strong identification of the domain of number with geometry, and geometry with physics, under the auspices of allegedly common structure proves to hinder the development of his science.

In this chapter, I want to examine Descartes's extension of physics to the functioning of the human body in the *Treatise of Man*. At the beginning of the book, he announces that he will describe the human body in abstraction from the soul, as if it were an 'earthen machine', similar to a clock, fountain, or mill. Its machinery is not the usual array of visible organs, but a series of microscopic mechanisms whose operations will explain all the corporeal activity that people share with animals who, according to Descartes, have no souls.[2]

Once again, Descartes is forced to revise his characterization of the simples of physics; he gives a surprising twist to the already vexed concept of subtle matter, and multiplies the varieties of third-element matter *ad libitum*. He must also revise the relational structure in which they stand, specifically, the quantified notion of machine. We have seen that for Descartes the paradigm of mechanical interaction is impact characterized by the invariant (bulk × speed), and that it is ambiguously indebted to the traditional, quantified theory of simple machines. Descartes treats the latter in terms of the invariant (weight × distance), and leaves unresolved how it is to be related to his vortex theory. But it is clearly in the background when he invokes and stretches the notion of machine for his extended physics.

These revisings and tacit annexations allow Descartes to appear to reduce what we would call psychology, biology, and biochemistry to physics. But they also cover over his violation of the requirements of method, that the simples and relational structure should remain fixed. Once again the method proves to be at odds with itself: the demands for homogeneity and for articulated hierarchy, like the demands for the transmission of truth and the extension of knowledge, cannot both be satisfied at once. And so too domains are conflated by Cartesian method before they have been sufficiently distinguished. The complex unities of psychology and biology thus never find an adequate representation in Descartes's account, and the alleged advance of scientific knowledge founders in conceptual confusion and *ad hoc* hypotheses. Descartes's mechanical description of the operations of the body, as well as the cognitive behaviour exhibited by animals, violates the order of reasons where it does not flatly reduce the domains of biology and psychology, folding them back into physics in a curious way.

THE MACHINE OF THE BODY

Descartes's attempt to extend physics to include biology hinges on the reappearance of first-element matter or subtle matter as 'animal spirits', the ability of third element matter to take on a variety of stable shapes and the ambiguity of the word 'machine', which Descartes turns to his own purposes. As in the earlier extensions of physics examined in the last three chapters, Descartes builds up a highly enriched version of material particles which far surpasses the earlier model of unity in virtue of geometrical shape or common motion; and he substitutes for the mechanism of impact a series of increasingly sophisticated relational structures which share the concept of machine only by the most elastic of analogies.

Many of the mechanisms Descartes invents in Part IV of the *Principles* involve particles of third-element matter, malleable agglomerations of first-element scrapings that take on and retain the shape of the solider, constraining second-element spheres in their environment.

Although these particles are much larger than the heavenly globules (second element matter), they cannot however be as solid or as capable of as much agitation. The fact that they have extremely irregular figures, less suited to movement than are the spherical figures of these globules, also contributes to this. For, inasmuch as the scrapings of which they are composed are joined together in innumerable diverse ways, it follows that these particles must differ very much from one another in size, solidity and figure; and that practically all of their shapes must be extremely irregular.[3]

The behaviour of oil is attributed to slender, branching particles and that of water to smooth and slippery particles. Magnetic phenomena are explained by the screw-shaped particles of the lodestone. Whence Descartes derives the initial malleability and the subsequent stability of these fanciful particles is not clear; it certainly cannot be deduced from his definition of material unity, even taken together with his definitions of liquids and solids. What links their shapes to their alleged causal efficacy is even less clear. And why such explanations should be called mechanical is murkier yet; the analogy to simple machines is barely discernible, and in any case the order of reasons is not supposed to proceed by analogy.

In some of the explanations given in the *Treatise of Man*, the mechanical analogy is clearer, though the fanciful details are no less unmotivated. Descartes's 'mechanical' model of the human body is a corpuscular version of Galenic physiology; once again Descartes has nothing to say about the medical tradition from which he has borrowed so much.[4] Subtle matter shows up as animal spirits, which circulate through the body carrying out various directive and regulatory functions. Indeed, animal spirits often look suspiciously like material stand-ins for the soul. Here is Descartes's account of breathing, much indebted to Galen's respiratory aerodynamics (Fig. 6.1).

Now in order to understand in detail how this machine (the body) breathes, imagine that muscle d is the one that serves to raise its chest or to lower its diaphragm, and that the muscle E is its opposite; and that the animal spirits that are in the brain cavity marked m flowing through the pore or little channel marked n, which naturally remains always open, proceed first to tube BF where, lowering the little membrane F, they cause the spirits to come from muscle E and inflate muscle d.

Next, reflect that around muscle d are certain membranes that press in on it more and more as it is increasingly inflated. The arrangement is such that, before all the spirits can pass from E to d, (the resistance caused by) these (membranes) stop(s) the flow (of spirits), causing them to be regorged, as it were, through BF. The result is that those from (nerve-) channel n are redirected. In this way, spirits proceed to cg and simultaneously force it open, causing muscle E to inflate and muscle d to deflate. This they continue to do as long as they are subject to the impetuosity of spirits tending to leave muscle d under pressure from the membranes that surround it; and when this impetuosity is spent, they resume their course through BF. Thus, ceaselessly the two muscles are made to inflate and deflate in turn. You must suppose this to be true as well of other muscles that serve the same end (breathing) and must reflect that they are so arranged that when muscles like d are inflated the space which contains the lungs is enlarged, and this causes air to come in as into a bellows when one expands it; and that when muscles contrary to d (are inflated) that space shrinks, and this causes the air to leave again.[5]

The picture that Descartes has sketched here is a kind of feedback mechanism, which is further compared to a bellows. While a

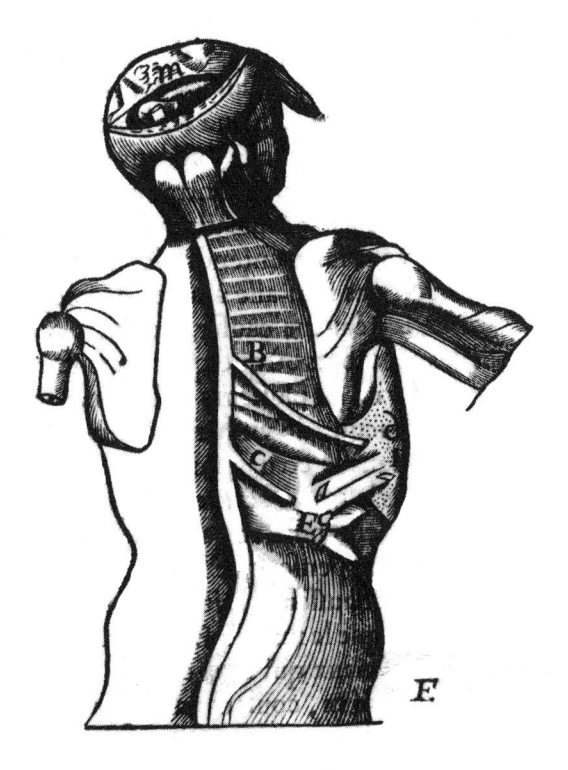

Fig. 6.1

bellows is a mechanical device, it certainly does not belong to the set of simple machines, and Descartes gives no suggestion of how its operation might be quantified. The notion of machine, here as elsewhere, is enlarged by analogy.

Descartes's biological mechanics thus depends in an unacknowledged way on the Galenic medical tradition and the classical theory of simple machines, and moreover builds on them by an imaginative set of similitudes very far from the rigorous deductions the original statement of method might lead one to expect. In the following passage, Descartes spells out his mechanical-biological simile in a way that, perhaps unwittingly, confesses the strong element of fantasy it involves.

And truly one can well compare the nerves of the machine that I am describing to the tubes of the mechanisms of these fountains, its muscles and tendons to divers other engines and springs which serve to move these mechanisms, its animal spirits to the water which drives them, of which the heart is the source and the brain's cavities the water main. Moreover, breathing and other such actions which are ordinary and natural to it, and which depend on the flow of the spirits, are like the movements of a clock or mill which the ordinary flow of water can render continuous. External objects which merely by their presence act on the organs of sense and by this means force them to move in several different ways, depending on how the parts of the brain are arranged, are like strangers who, entering some of the grottoes of these fountains, unwittingly cause the movements that then occur, since they cannot enter without stepping on certain tiles so arranged that, for example, if they approach a Diana bathing they will cause her to hide in the reeds; and if they pass farther to pursue her they will cause a Neptune to advance and menace them with his trident; or if they go in another direction they will make a marine monster come out and spew water into their faces, or other such things according to the whims of the engineers who made them.[6]

For any given new phenomena, physical, biological, or psychological, Descartes seems to feel free to coin new particles and new machines, that is, new simples and new relational structures. The fixed originating basis stipulated by method appears to have been left far behind, as well as the initial link with mathematics.

THE BRAIN

In the *Treatise of Man*, Descartes not only describes the functioning of muscles, digestion, respiration, and so forth, but devotes many pages to the operations of the brain as well. His description of human reflex action and of animal behaviour, I would argue, models activity which looks very much like cognition. In order to construct a model of entities and actions of such complexity and intentionality, Descartes attributes a surprising array of new characteristics to matter. It is tempting to say that he spiritualizes matter, despite his dualism and the exigencies of his method.

The strict distinction between *res cogitans* and *res extensa* not only plays an important role in the unfolding of the argument of the *Meditations,* but also serves as a methodological rule for science: do not attribute psychological features to the objects of study, or use them for explanatory purposes. That the objects of science, the machines of nature, do not have feelings or intentions proves to be a useful rule which allows Descartes to guard against many of the errors of Renaissance Naturalism.[7] But clearly Descartes wants to throw the net of his mechanical philosophy very widely, to include not only physics but biology as well. His physiological mechanics in the *Treatise of Man* rejects the soul as a principle of explanation for nutritive, sensitive, and motive activity in living things, and instead explains these functions in terms of corpuscular and microscopic mechanisms.

Descartes does not see this mechanical modelling as a subversion of his dualism, for he denies that cognition is involved in the behaviour of soulless animals. However, even a number of his contemporaries disagreed with him on this point. Gassendi, for example, argues in the fifth set of *Objections*,

> Look to it, nevertheless, that that sensation which exists in the brutes, since it is not dissimilar to your sensation, be not capable of earning the title of thought also, and that thus the brutes themselves may have a mind not dissimilar to your own.
>
> You will say, I, holding the citadel in the brain, receive whatsover is sent me by the (animal) spirits which permeate the nerves, and thus the act of sense which is said to be effected by the whole body is transacted in my presence. Good; but in the brutes, there are nerves, (animal) spirits, a brain, and a conscious principle residing therein, which in a similar manner receives the messages sent by the animal spirits and accomplishes the act of sensation.[8]

Gassendi's point is that much of the biological activity that Descartes reconstructs in purely mechanical terms has an irreducible cognitive dimension. And I want to show that Descartes's attempt to model cognition in mechanical terms radically transforms his original notions of matter and machine.

In Descartes's corpuscular version of the Galenic tradition, the heart is a kind of furnace where God has kindled 'one of those fires without light'. It accelerates and rarefies particles in the blood which it pumps straight up into the pineal gland, converting the blood to animal spirits which then pour continuously out of the pineal. Furnaces and pumps are two more mechanical devices, not included in the classical canon of simple machines, that Descartes borrows by analogy. And he invokes the first and second laws of motion in the explanation of why rarefied blood should mount to the brain.

All the liveliest, strongest and subtlest parts of this blood proceed to the cavities of the brain, inasmuch as the arteries that bring them there are the ones that come in the straightest line from the heart; and, as you know, all bodies in motion tend in so far as possible to continue moving in a straight line.[9]

The animal spirits that do not make it up to the brain find their way to the 'vessels designed for generation', where their metaphoric qualities of quickness and liveliness are presumably germane. Fig. 6.2 illustrates this situation.[10] Descartes continues:

As for those parts of the blood that penetrate as far as the brain, they serve not only to nourish and sustain its substance, but also and principally to

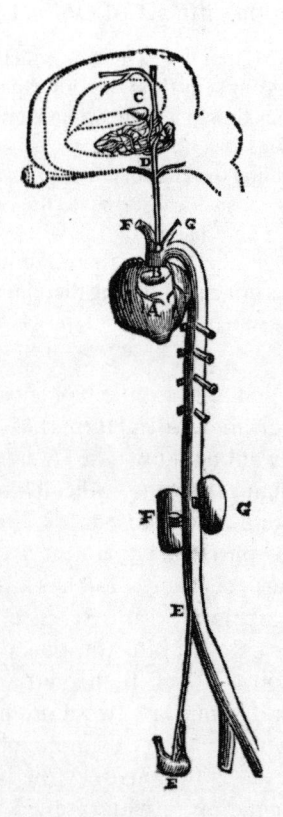

Fig. 6.2

Descartes's Physiology

produce there a certain very subtle wind, or rather a very lively and very pure flame, which is called the 'animal spirits'. For one must know that the arteries that bring blood from the heart, having divided into an infinity of little branches and having composed the little tissues that are stretched like tapestries at the bottom of the concavities of the brain (the choroid plexus), reassemble around a certain little gland (the pineal) situated near the middle of the brain's substance just at the entrance to its cavities.[11]

The animal spirits enter the pineal, which Descartes compares to a 'very full-flowing spring', and then pour out of it in every direction, entering, through pores in the internal surface of the brain ventricle, the nerves which lead to all the members of the body (Fig. 6.3). (Fountains here enter the list of mechanical devices.) The quickness and subtlety with which the animal spirits have been endowed give them an ambiguous directive function; entering the nerves in patterned ways, they produce appropriate bodily activity.

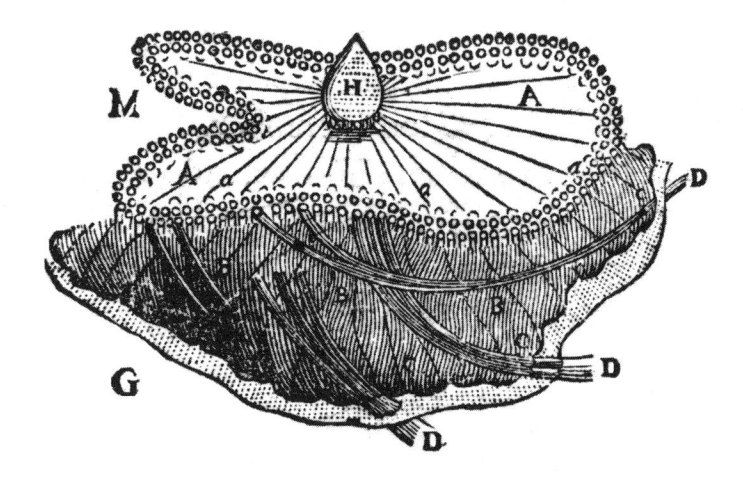

Fig. 6.3

This causal pathway plays an important role in Descartes's account of animal and human reflex action, where the corporeal machine allegedly acts independently of the soul. The following passage is from Descartes's reply to Arnauld's misgivings, in the fourth set of *Objections*, about his causal model of perception.

When a man in falling thrusts out his hand to save his head he does that without his reason counselling him so to act, but merely because the sight of the impending fall penetrating to his brain, drives the animal spirits into the nerves in the manner necessary for this motion, and for producing it without the mind's desiring it, and as though it were the working of a machine. Now, when we experience this as a fact in ourselves, why should we marvel so greatly if the light reflected from the body of a wolf into the eyes of a sheep should be equally capable of exciting in it the motion of flight.[12]

An external object, Descartes claims, sets up certain diverse motions in the 'intervening transparent medium', which in turn set up diverse motions in the little filaments of our nerves. These correspondingly open in diverse ways the pores of the brain, that is, the openings of the nerve fibres which compose the internal surface of the brain ventricle. The pineal gland, pouring forth animal spirits, sits opposite this surface, which receives the flow of animal spirits from the surface of the pineal gland itself. Consequently, changes in the openness and orientation of the brain-tubules' openings will change the pattern of flow from the pineal as well.[13]

Descartes's description of the mutual adjustment of brain patterns and pineal patterns is really a highly sophisticated feedback mechanism. The flow of animal spirits back into the brain runs through the nerves out to the muscles of the extremities and directs motor response by paired contractions of the muscles.[14] In the particular case of vision, retinal patterns play an important intermediary role in transmitting the diverse motions which code colour, form, and distance to the nerve fibres of the brain.[15] And finally, the patterned flow of animal spirits through the fibres of the brain may induce certain more or less permanent configurations in the fibres; these 'folds' are corporeal memory, which in turn influences the subsequent course of animal spirits.[16]

Clearly, the important phrase in Descartes's account of these processes is 'diverse or patterned motion'. Such motion constitutes information about the external world on the way into the brain, and the interpretation of it, as appropriate response, on the way out. Neither uniform nor random motion is a likely candidate for embodied information or directives; informative motion must be diverse, and indeed diverse in patterned ways. Descartes wants to make of the (so far soulless) pineal gland a locus for complex algorithms which convert perceptual patterns into patterns inducing movement.

A number of difficulties arise from Descartes's attempt to model animal and human reflex action in terms of his mechanical, corpuscular physics. Given the nature of his undertaking, he must negotiate three distinct levels of description, the physical, the biological, and the psychological. The testimony of twentieth-century science is that the relations between these levels are problematic and unclear. At the very least one can say that these relations are not reductive in any simple sense, and that no isomorphisms can be given to correlate entities and processes of one level with those of another. Rather, the task for the sciences (one which has proved very fruitful for research) has been to hypothesize what are at best indeterminate and many-many correlations between the terms of descriptive levels, and to see how those hypotheses are borne out in empirical research.[17]

One can hardly expect Descartes to have foreseen the immense complexity of this undertaking. However, I would urge that his methodological penchant for conceiving the enlargement of scientific knowledge as the construction of new complexes from homogeneous terms associated by a single, transparent relational structure is unfortunate in the context of this problem. For it leads him to regard his biological work as a straightforward extension of his physical principles to new areas of research, and blinds him both to their inadequacy for the task, and to his covert revision of them as he strives to make them adequate. In other words, he cannot recognize methodologically the extent to which he is negotiating heterogeneous levels of description in the *Treatise of Man*, and not a homogeneous field of facts about matter in motion.

In Descartes's physics, all causal interaction is the impact of one bit of matter on another; the interaction is linear—one cause produces one effect—and deterministic. No room exists in this analysis for the notion of pattern which is so central to Descartes's cognitive physiology. Thus he must either revise or short-circuit his original conception of causal interaction to deal with the kinds of biological and psychological phenomena addressed in the *Treatise of Man*. Neither strategy can be recognized for what it is.

In his description of the eye, the pineal, the ventricular lining of the brain, and the animal spirits, Descartes employs both strategies. On the one hand, he invents feedback mechanisms which are not linear and deterministic, reducible to relations of impact, or quantifiable by means of the mathematics he knows, to explain the mutual regulation of pineal and ventricular patterns, and the animal spirits they organize. That is, Descartes may have located certain biological 'mechanisms', but they are like impact or the simple machines only by a highly attenuated analogy which itself demands, but never receives, analysis and justification.

On the other hand, he simply suspends the causal chain at certain crucial points, and injects a non-causal, cognitive term (God) into his account. Specifically, the pineal gland and the texture of the brain filaments are given the function of converting patterns of animal spirits which carry information about the environment in appropriate ways to patterns of animal spirits which will direct muscular function, i.e. actions. This conversion process looks suspiciously like intelligence, and indeed is attributed to God: God constructs animals with suitable pineal and ventricular 'programmes'.

As to the arrangements of the filaments that compose the brain substance, it is either acquired or natural (innate) . . . (First, then,) to explain what the natural arrangements consist in. Know that in forming the filaments God arranged them as follows. The passages that He left among them are able to conduct the spirits, when these are moved by a particular (stimulant) action, towards nerves that permit just those movements in this machine that a similar action could incite in us when we act through natural instincts.[18]

At the biological level, Descartes introduces mechanisms which cannot be construed, in his original terms, as mathematical-physical. At the psychological level, he introduces a cognizer (God) for the consciousness that is missing in his soulless animal-machines.

From the epistemological point of view, Descartes's strategies raise a further quandary. In the *Treatise of Man*, ideas are materialized, and thus hypostatized with a vengeance, for Descartes equates ideas with patterned flows of animal spirits.[19] He claims a correspondence between patterns of the external object, retinal patterns, patterns in the ventricular lining, and patterns of flow of the animal spirits through the surface of the pineal and then warns,

Now among these figures, it is not those imprinted on the organs of external sense, or on the internal surface of the brain, but only those traced in spirits on the surface of gland H [the pineal], *where the seat of imagination and common sense is*, that should be taken to be ideas, that is to say, to be the forms or images which the rational soul will consider directly when, being united to this machine, it will imagine or will sense any object.[20]

Such material ideas then became proxy-objects; they are what the soul knows directly, and raise a sceptical worry about the knower's access to the external world. At the same time, Descartes is trading on the ambiguity of his notion of animal spirits, to which he has assigned spiritual functions within the corporeal machine. On the one hand, they are 'nothing but' aggregates of bits of matter in motion and so are the subject of physics. On the other hand, they are active and patterned, conveying information on the way in and directing action on the way out; they embody both information and intelligence. Their ambiguity thus allows Descartes to move between distinct levels of description, and incidentally to violate the order of reasons, without acknowledging explicitly that he does so.

As physical objects, animal spirits interact with the pineal in a fashion which seems to be causal; according to the *Principles*, that interaction must be a spatially located series of collisions. But in the *Principles*, objects which collide are causally efficacious not because they are patterned, but because they are matter in motion. Only if cognition is construed as a causal chain linking the external object to a part of the brain does the pineal pattern seem to be a proxy-object. But a description of this causal chain cannot include terms like 'pattern' which are irrelevant to Descartes's account of physical causation.

By introducing the term 'pattern', Descartes shifts the level of description to the biological and even the psychological. If animal spirits impinge on (*faire sentir*) the soul (finally reinstated by Descartes and located in the pineal) in virtue of being patterned, it is the patterning which is consequential for knowledge and that consequentiality is not the causality of Cartesian physics. Patterns *qua* patterns cannot be physically-causally transmitted, by means of collisions; to account for their transmission, one must appeal to a revised and extended notion of causality appropriate to biology, which is in fact what Descartes often tries to do. And if animal spirits embody the recognition of environmental features and appropriate action in response to them, Descartes has shifted the level of description to the psychological. At that level, for a pattern to be consequential it must be recognized as such, interpreted, cognitively grasped, by a consciousness; in effect it is information about the environment for an animal that has intentions and projects, albeit in a rudimentary way.[21]

Descartes invokes this level in his remarks about the wolf and the sheep cited earlier, only to claim that it can be reduced unproblematically to physical-causal terms. Arnauld finds his claim unfounded and highly problematic;[22] in a sense I have been trying to explicate Arnauld's uneasiness. Descartes simply cannot recover such phenomena from the simples and relational structures of the *Principles*; instead, his biology revises or circumvents his physics, and generates in addition problematic results for epistemology.

By contrast, my own contention is that the descriptive level of psychology, while it need not dispense with references to causal interaction at the physical and biological level, should subsume them to its own account. This subordination will be a series of hypotheses about how items and processes peculiar to the various sciences are correlated, and its details are worked out piecemeal in empirical research. The relation which psychology delineates between a creature and its environment should be cognitive, intentional, localized in an only indeterminate way, non-linear, and direct. My claim may seem anachronistic in this context. But in fact the kinds of mistakes Descartes makes by confounding levels of description also permeate contemporary materialist accounts in epistemology and cognitive psychology.

A final difficulty remains with the earthen machine which for Descartes constitutes an animal or the human body without its soul. What kind of unity can it have? The simple machines have a mathematical unity conferred on them by the invariants which characterize them: a balance counts as one thing because the product of the weight on one arm and the length of the arm is always equal to the same product taken on the other arm. For thus a change in one part exacts a compensating change in another part. Likewise, what makes a system where two bodies collide one thing is the invariant mv. But the biological mechanisms invented by Descartes in the *Treatise of Man* have moved so far from the original simile with mathematics that no analogous principle of unity can be found for them. Why the congeries of microscopic and macroscopic machines that compose the body should hang together as one organism is no clearer than why the spherical particles of second-element matter, or the multiform particles of third-element matter persist as unities. In the next chapter, I suggest that the problem of unity reasserts itself with respect to the soul in the *Meditations*.

Notes

1. For a detailed description of these issues, see Clarke, *Descartes' Philosophy of Science*, chs. 5 and 6; and G. Hatfield, 'First Philosophy and Natural Philosophy in Descartes' in A. J. Holland (ed.) *Philosophy, Its History and Historiography* (Dordrecht: D. Reidel, 1985), 149–64.
2. Descartes wrote the *Traité de l'Homme* as the second part of his treatise *Le Monde*. It was published posthumously by Claude Clerselier, as *L'Homme de René Descartes* (Paris, 1664). I use the translation and commentary given in *Treatise of Man*, ed. T. S. Hall (Cambridge, Mass.: Harvard University Press, 1972). For each citation, I will give first the page numbers in Hall and then the page numbers from vol. xi. 119–202 of Adam and Tannery, where it is reprinted.
3. *Principia Philosophiae*, pp. 184; 206.
4. Hall's running commentary, given in the extensive footnotes to his edition of the *Treatise of Man*, indicates in detail Descartes's debt to Galen.
5. *Traité de l'Homme*, pp. 30–2; 138–40.
6. Ibid. 22; 131–2.
7. Richard Westfall makes this argument in *The Construction of Modern Science* (New York: John Wiley & Sons, 1971), ch. 2.
8. HR ii. 144–5; AT vii. 268–9.
9. *Traité de l'Homme*, pp. 17; 128.
10. Ibid.
11. Ibid., text, 19–20; 128; diagram, 83; 174.
12. HR ii. 103–4; AT vii. 229–30.
13. *Traité de l'Homme*, pp. 77–82; 170–4.
14. Ibid. 21–30; 130–9.
15. Ibid. 49–68; 151–63. Also, 94–102; 182–92.
16. Ibid. 87–90; 176–9.
17. A great deal has been written on this topic in recent discussion of scientific reduction. Especially interesting sources include S. O. Kimbrough, 'On the Reduction of Genetics to Molecular Biology', *Philosophy of Science*, 46 (1979), 389–406, and Maull, 'Unifying Science Without Reduction'.
18. *Traité de l'Homme*, pp. 103–4; 192–3.
19. Ibid. 86–8; 176–8.
20. Ibid. 86; 176.
21. Some of my theoretical orientation is drawn from J. J. Gibson, *The Ecological Approach to Visual Perception* (Boston: Houghton Mifflin Co., 1979).

22. HR ii. 85–6; AT vii. 204–5. J. Yolton has an interesting but quite different account of the relation of Descartes to Arnauld on these matters in *Perceptual Acquaintance from Descartes to Reid* (Minneapolis: University of Minnesota Press, 1984), ch. 1.

7
The *Meditations* Re-examined

IN the previous six chapters, I have discussed Cartesian method as an intuitionist and reductive way of constructing subject-matters: the problems of geometry from relations of proportionality among straight line segments; the complex items of the physical cosmos from bits of matter in uniform, rectilinear motion. And I have mentioned in passing that the *Meditations* is designed to inaugurate and ground these projects by employing the method in a 'peculiarly pure' manner. Does this mean that the *Meditations* has no subject-matter? Or if it does, what could that be?

In this final chapter, I want to argue that in the *Meditations* Descartes employs his method to reconstruct the human self as knower, beginning from the 'simple' condition of pure self-consciousness where the only content of thought is the self's activity of thinking, and ending with a complex self confidently prepared to take up the investigation of natural science and human happiness. According to Descartes, the purpose of a human being is to carry out the activity of knowing in the proper way; the *Meditations*, presenting and instantiating the order of reasons, offers the requisite self-knowledge for this end.

My interpretation of the *Meditations* is therefore distinct from and somewhat at odds with the current tendency among contemporary Anglo-American philosophers to read it first and foremost as Descartes's attempt to ensure the certainty of knowledge. Their commentaries thus by and large scrutinize the inferential relations among various propositions asserted throughout the six meditations.[1] Considerations of certainty are obviously important to Descartes's undertaking in the *Meditations*, but I see the unity and competence of the knowing human self as the central issue. The simples of the *Meditations* are not propositions; Descartes was far too distrustful of and alienated from Scholastic logic for such a reading to be plausible. Rather, they are clear and distinct ideas, 'atoms of evidence', which are both activities of the human knower and representations of things.[2]

Descartes the intuitionist rejects a correspondence theory of truth in the sense of the dogmatic Aristotelian or Thomistic adequation of proposition and thing. For an intuitionist, knowledge cannot be abstracted from the knowing subject and our ways of coming to know the object according to a canon. Thus a philosophical psychology or anthropology will be central to any intuitionist metaphysics, as well as an explication of the canon.[3] The *Meditations* performs both these functions. Moreover, an intuitionist in general denies that the existence of an object can be asserted independently of the mode of its construction in thought. But Descartes should not therefore be seen as an idealist or as espousing a coherence theory of truth. Ideas are representations for Descartes, and in Meditation III the knower confronts an idea, the idea of God, that clearly and distinctly surpasses all his powers of construction. Its very transcendence reveals that what it represents exists, and in turn guarantees the existence of all things represented by clear and distinct ideas.[4]

My criticisms of the *Meditations* will thus not involve a logical reconstruction of Descartes's arguments, or go back over the issue of the Cartesian circle. Rather, I find difficulties in the *Meditations* analogous to those generated by Descartes's reductionist procedures in the *Geometry*, the *Principles*, and the *Treatise of Man*. Throughout this book, I have argued that Descartes's reductionist method, while allowing him to open up new avenues of research and to integrate previously isolated domains, is none the less deeply flawed, for it leads him to misconstrue or close off prematurely his own innovations. Believing that his method is both ampliative and truth-preserving, he often regards hasty generalizations and unfounded analogies as validated. His allegiance to homogeneous starting-points and univocal abstract structures prevents him from understanding his new domains as combinations of partially distinct domains partially unified by hypothesis. He has trouble accounting for the unity of his simples as well as his complexes: the simples dissolve into relational structure, and the complexes dissolve into the simples. And his insistence on intuition as providing radical starting-points for a process of elaboration that unfolds out of them keeps him from acknowledging the rich traditions, geometric, mechanical, and medical, in which his work is embedded, or his exclusions and debts with respect to them.

Similarly, in the *Meditations* the simplicity and homogeneity of the starting-points leads to a serious impoverishment of the subject-matter, the human self. And where Descartes attempts to enrich his account of the self, he imports, often from unacknowledged tradition, extra structure to which he is not strictly entitled, in violation of the order of reasons. The unity of the *cogito* at the beginning of the *Meditations* remains insufficiently examined, and the unity of the complex self at the end remains unstable, in constant danger of dissolution. This instability mirrors the superficial, *ad hoc* character of Descartes's unification of theology and materialist natural philosophy in his dualist metaphysics. In the next section I will briefly review the argument of the *Meditations*, following to a certain extent Gueroult's assertion that it unfolds according to the order of reasons. Then I will examine some of Descartes's difficulties in maintaining the unity of the human self, finally focusing my conclusions by a critique of his account of how we come to know extension.

THE ARGUMENT OF THE *MEDITATIONS*

Descartes transposes the concept of method from the mathematical to the metaphysical in order to characterize, ground, and extend knowledge, including mathematics, in the *Meditations*. Even though heuristically mathematics may have suggested his method to Descartes, he makes it clear that mathematics cannot ground itself; the first principles in the single order of reasons that constitutes all of human knowledge must arise from the mind's scrutiny of its own activity. The hyperbolic doubt reveals the essence of the human self as pure self-consciousness, 'I am, I think', the residue of a series of eliminations of all conditioned knowledge, even mathematics.[5]

In the moment of illumination in Meditation II, the self knows the real, not merely modal, distinction between spirit and matter, for it sees itself essentially as the activity of thought and nothing more. Indeed, it sorts out the extent of its subjective certainty by a series of distinctions, of what excludes what. Considering the piece of wax, it excludes all the testimony of sensation except the mathematical invariants which are the abstract condition of its representation of the wax; but its knowledge of mathematical extension here, like its assurance of its own existence, has so far only subjective necessity. Self-consciousness and mathematics in Meditation II are purely abstract conditions of any possible science.[6]

And thus it seems that Descartes, as paradigmatic knower, must exclude from himself everything that is not thought, to discover his true self. Beginning with the (metaphysical) unit, the *cogito*, Descartes uses what he takes to be ampliative deduction to construct links of (metaphysical) proportionality between one clear and distinct idea and the next: the *cogito*, God, the mathematicals, and quantified *res extensa*.[7] The view of knowledge that emerges is intuitionist and critical, in accord with Descartes's view of mathematics. He is an intuitionist in that he reduces the true to the evident. The criterion by which he judges a given claim to be true is whether, when contemplated by an undistracted and unprejudiced mental vision, it is clear and distinct, thus compelling assent. Descartes converts this epistemic necessity from the merely subjective to the objective in Meditation III by inferring from the idea of God, God's existence and perfection, so that He can serve as the guarantor of clear and distinct ideas. This epistemology is apriorist, for the kind of warranting process it invokes makes no appeal to human experience as grounds for invalidating clear and distinct ideas.

The critical import of Descartes's epistemology stems from intuition so conceived, for what is clear and distinct stands in finite, exact proportion to the *cogito* and is homogeneous with it. Human knowledge is delineated as a finite and homogeneous nexus of clear and distinct ideas, which excludes the infinitary and indeterminate. In other words, part of correct method for Descartes is to see clearly and distinctly where the boundaries of the clear and distinct lie. This critical thrust would push Cartesian epistemology towards idealism, since the human mind knows only what is homogeneous with it, that is, finitary ideas, except that Descartes counteracts this tendency by appealing to the alterity of God, whose reality is infinite, as an independent source (and as the guarantor of other independent sources) of ideas.

Indeed, the success of Descartes's attempt to argue from the order of knowing to the order of being in the *Meditations* hinges on the knowing self's encounter with idea-terms that appear to be disproportionate to it: in Meditation III the idea of God whose objective reality is infinite, and in Meditation VI the ideas of sense whose objective reality is , as it were, infinitesimal.[8] The infinity of the idea of God, together with Descartes's principle that there must be as much formal reality in the cause of an idea as the idea has objective reality, entails that God is genuinely alterior to the self. Ideas for Descartes are effects of causes and they are representative

The Meditations Re-examined

of objects beyond themselves; as entities they have formal reality, as representative they have objective reality. The infinity of the idea of God entails both that its cause is something other than and disproportionately superior to the *cogito*, and that it is a faithful picture of its archetype, for only one thing can be the absolute maximum of formal reality depicted in the objective reality of the idea of God. The human knower can infer from it not only that something alterior exists, but precisely what that something is. In the special case of the idea of God, the principle of causality and the epistemological principle of correspondence come to the same thing, and so the idea of God exhibits complete objective validity.[9]

God's existence and perfection, His revealed characteristics, then guarantee the objective validity of all clear and distinct ideas, first and foremost the mathematicals. The mathematicals, like all other ideas, are representative, but according to Descartes in Meditation V they are caused by something with a finite amount of objective reality, and represent rational realities or essences. They are faithful pictures of these archetypes, which exist independently of both the soul of the knower and of nature, *res extensa*. For external nature is introduced subsequently to the justification of mathematical ideas in the order of reasons.[10]

In Meditation VI, the mathematicals are shown to be not merely subjective but objective conditions for the self's experience of the external world and for the possibility of science. They are applicable to the ideas of sense, whose objective reality hovers between being and nothingness, and thus save sensation from absolute unintelligibility. Sensations are ideas, but their vexed representative function is destined always to remain somewhat obscure and confused. The self experiences the ideas of sense as a passion; since their infinitesimal reality cannot appropriately be ascribed to God, and since God is not a deceiver, they can be assumed to proceed from a material realm alterior to both God and the self.[11] This realm is jointly mastered by the mathematicals, and by a psycho-physiological account of how to assess the intrinsic error which permeates the ideas of sense.

Clearly, my recapitulation of the *Meditations* owes much to Gueroult's reading, but this debt is intentional. Since among modern scholars, Gueroult best succeeds in doing justice to the integrity of Descartes's project in the *Meditations*, I want to direct my criticisms in the next two sections against that reading, in the hope that I will thereby not take Descartes to task for trivial or superficial reasons.

THE UNITY OF THE HUMAN SELF

In Meditation II, when Descartes as exemplary knower has had his moment of illumination, discovering that his act of asserting 'I know, I am' is inalienable even in the face of hyperbolic doubt, he undertakes an inventory of his soul. 'But what then am I? A thing which thinks. What is a thing which thinks? It is a thing which doubts, understands, [conceives], affirms, denies, wills, refuses, which also imagines and feels.'[12] The unity of the *cogito*, where the I affirms only itself, where the idea as activity and as representative contents coincide, where thought and existence are one, is very impressive. And yet when the thinker examines this moment of subjective unity, it immediately opens to reveal a multiplicity of functions. Although the *cogito* momentarily abstracts from the diversity of contents in ideas, it cannot altogether abstract from this diversity of functions, and is articulated into a collection of faculties, intellect, will, imagination, memory, and sensation. (The doctrine of faculties is borrowed from a long-standing philosophical and medical tradition, which Descartes once again does not acknowledge.)

To bring this encapsulated diversity of functions into harmonious interrelation is Descartes's intention as he, the thinker, pursues the order of reasons step by step. The intuitionist's criterion for knowledge, confirmation according to a canon, requires an orderly relationship among the faculties. Thus Descartes shows that infinitary will must be subordinate to finitary intellect, passive sense must be mastered by active imagination, and imagination and memory in turn must submit to the discipline of intellect. But Descartes's hierarchy of faculties is unstable, and fails to produce a convincing unity within the knowing self.

In Cartesian metaphysics, spirit is the category not only of activity but also of unity and self-sameness in the strongest sense. And the *cogito*, the moment in which the self knows itself with subjective certainty as pure spirit, is the absolute starting-point for the analytic order of reasons. Thus Descartes never supposes that the unity of the *cogito* might be impugned, and might need to be revised in light of developments later on in the order of reasons. Analogously, he never remarks that the unexamined unity of line lengths has been profoundly transformed by the end of the *Geometry* to become the multivalent functional interdependence of a hybrid curve-equation, or that the complex systems of the *Principles* reveal the inadequacy of material unity conceived as common motion.

By contrast, matter is the category of the 'passive and inert' and of '*partes extra partes*'.[13] (One reason why Descartes has so much trouble finding models of material unity in the *Principles* is that all unity must be imported one way or another from the category of spirit.) When in Meditation II Descartes has unpacked the *cogito* into a collection of faculties, he is right away troubled by sense and imagination, for they present corporeal things as more distinctly known than spirit. Their insistent representations thus threaten the order of reasons. At this point, Descartes takes up his well-known consideration of the piece of wax and concludes that only intellect, not imagination or sense, can reveal to him what wax in general is. Still under the shadow of the hyperbolic doubt, he may be deceived in believing that external, corporeal objects exist and that he is truly employing the faculties of sense and imagination. But his subjective certainty that he thinks, that he employs the faculty of intellect, and that the mathematical idea of extension grasped by the intellect is the subjective condition for any possible acquaintance with material objects, remains intact.[14]

Descartes's reflections in Meditation II establish the substantial distinction between body and soul: soul is essentially distinct from body, known prior to and more easily than body. But this distinction, so sharply drawn, also then threatens the unity of the faculties, for those most closely associated with body do not seem to belong to the true self in the same way as the purely spiritual faculty of intellect. If no proportion holds between soul and body, how can one hold between the representational contents of pure idea and sensation, or between the faculties of intellect and sensation?

The understanding or intellect is purely spiritual; imagination, memory, and sensation are increasingly corporeal, in the metaphoric sense that they depend upon or are orientated towards the body. Imagination and memory are actions that require certain concomitant processes to take place in the body, and Descartes characterizes sensation as a passive reaction to bodily changes. Thus the bipolar opposition body–soul is figuratively reproduced in the soul itself and the faculties are ordered along its axis. But then the lack of proportion between the body and soul threatens the integrity of the self. Can such a heterogeneous plurality of faculties constitute a unity? If not, can the intellect alone constitute the self? Then what is the status of the other faculties? does Descartes intend to invoke all the faculties as an articulation of the self-reflexive moment of the *cogito*, or identify the self of the *cogito* with the intellect alone?

Descartes is equivocal on this issue. At first in Meditation II, he asserts that sensation, like taking nourishment and walking, does not truly belong to what he is; only thinking does, that is, only the faculty of intellect.[15] Indeed, Descartes sometimes tends to segregate sensation by intellectualizing the ambiguous middle faculties of imagination and memory, as if the self could quite well employ the latter even if it did not happen to have a body. In various letters, he proposes a second, intellectual memory; and Meditation V can be read as suggesting that our imaginative grasp of mathematical ideas need not depend on the body.[16] But shortly after his isolation of sensation as an alienable faculty in Meditation II, he unpacks the *cogito* as the full spectrum of faculties, claiming that even if none of his imaginings and sensings is true, he still has the powers of imagining and sensing, and they form part of and are nothing other than his thought.[17]

In the fifth set of *Objections*, Gassendi calls Descartes on precisely this point in his commentary relative to Meditation II. He notes in section 3, 'You proceed to say that, of the things ascribed to soul, neither nourishment nor walking belong to you. . . . You proceed, saying that you are without sensation . . .',[18] and a little later in section 7 makes the following observations:

'But', you ask, 'what then am I? A thing which thinks. What is a thing which thinks? It is a thing which doubts, understands, affirms, denies, wills, refuses, which also imagines and feels.' You mention many things here which in themselves cause me no difficulty. This alone makes me pause, your saying you are a thing which feels. It is indeed strange, for you had previously maintained the opposite; or perchance did you mean that in addition to yourself there is a corporeal faculty residing in the eye, in the ear, and in the other organs, which receiving the semblance of things, gives rise to the act of sensation in a way that allows you thereupon to complete it, and brings it to pass that you are really the very self which sees, hears, and perceives other things? It is for this reason, in my opinion, that you make sensation as well as imagination a species of thought.[19]

Descartes's reply to this objection is only to reiterate the real distinction between body and soul, and his claim that the mind can act independently of the brain. 'The whole nature of the mind consists in thinking, while the whole nature of the body consists in being an extended thing, and . . . there is nothing at all common to thought and extension.'[20] But the thrust of Gassendi's objection is not so much how mind and brain are or are not related, but how the faculties are related to the self. He sees that the self as an ordered collection of faculties is in danger of decomposition.

Gueroult explicates this section by admitting that there is a distinction between the intellect and the other faculties, but it is nothing like the distinction which severs body from soul. Descartes intends the latter to be a real distinction between substances, whereas the former is only modal.

Since I cannot know myself except through intelligence [intellect], I see immediately that I am only intelligence; and because I am only intelligence, intelligence alone, and not imagination and sense, is capable of allowing me to know what I am. That is why I must conclude that imagination and sense are alien to the nature of my mind, while intelligence, which alone is required in order to understand it, belongs to it alone.

Is that to say that intelligence must exclude imagination and sense from my nature in the same way that it excludes body itself from it? No, for imagination and sensation are grasped directly in my mind as thoughts, while body is outside the mind and is unknown to me. Imagination and sense must therefore be related to the soul in so far as they cannot be understood without it. They can therefore not be excluded from it in the same way that the body is excluded from it; but, being alien to its nature, they can be related to it only as contingent properties, at least with respect to that in which they differ from intelligence. They are modes of my soul, and there is only a modal difference between my soul and them.[21]

Gueroult, insisting on the order of reasons, interprets Descartes as claiming that the faculties of sensing, desiring, remembering, and imagining are thus only contingent, not essential, properties of the self. Their dependence on the body renders them alien to the self grasped in the moment of truth in Meditation II: I think, I am.

Descartes has then two possible ways of treating the faculties. If he acknowledges their diversity *ab initio* as he tries to establish harmonious interrelations among them, he will violate the order of reasons by invoking the body too early, long before Meditation VI. A self possessed of imagination, memory, and especially sense must also come equipped with a body; the modal distinctions among the faculties are inexplicable and unmotivated without the substantial distinction between body and soul and the existence of body. But what can hold such a self together, before the introduction of the 'substantial unity' of body and soul in Meditation VI? Intellect seems to float above the other faculties, in spite of its alleged directive functions.

If on the other hand Descartes tries to remain true to the order of reasons, he must spiritualize and assimilate imagination and memory back into intellect, and leave sensation as a separate and anomalous faculty. Then the demand for homogeneity wins out: the articulation of the *cogito* into faculties seems unnecessary, and the self has no reason to acknowledge sensation as its own. And this angelic decomposition leaves the self stranded in universality, for the *cogito* is not only the simplest but the most universal condition for knowledge. The thinker's self-knowledge of his true self is cut off from the dimension of particularity that the corporeal faculties of memory, imagination, and sense might provide.[22]

The shadow of the real, substantial distinction between *res cogitans* and *res extensa* falls on the Cartesian self and threatens it with a disruption that the abstract unity of spirit may not redeem. What kind of self could experience its memory and desire, to say nothing of its perception and imagining, as alien and as merely contingent? For such a self, history and moral experience, its own projects, gratifications, regrets, and creaturely habits would play no role in the constitution of its true self. Even the pilgrim souls in Augustine and Dante, merely passing through on their way to transcendence, are not so thoroughly stripped of their earthly particularity.

THE PUZZLE OF *RES EXTENSA*

In Meditation III, Descartes tries to take inventory of the sorts of ideas with which he finds his mind to be occupied. The diversity of ideas is quite different from the diversity of faculties, and yet Descartes identifies certain ideas as immediately derivable from his idea of himself, that is, from the self-reflexive moment of the *cogito*: 'substance, duration, number and such like.'[23] (In a letter to Clerselier (23 April 1649)[24] he mentions that he could have added truth, perfection, and order.) But the idea of extension, he has to admit, is

The Meditations Re-examined

not formally in him. How is it that extension appears to be one of his innate ideas? Having excluded external nature in Meditation I, is the thinker entitled to invoke the idea of purely mathematical extension in Meditation II and again in Meditation V? Does extension belong to the category of spirit or of matter? And then is he really entitled to reinstate material *res extensa*, using the bridges of God and mathematics in Meditation VI?

Gueroult argues that Descartes's discussion of the piece of wax in Meditation II establishes the subjective necessity of the mathematical idea of extension as an abstract condition of the possibility of the representation of external objects. The mathematical invariants which Descartes points to there are rules that make possible the reidentification of an object as such under all the metamorphoses of sensation; they are principles of unity for thought.

The idea of extension escapes the doubt of the evil genius, for even if it is intrinsically false, that would not prevent it from necessarily governing my representation of the corporeal object and establishing its unity and permanence under the changing diversity of its sensible covering ... but the reality of extension, as essence or as existence, remains doubtful.[25]

The innate idea of extension founds the unity and permanence of the representation of objects because it allows the thinker to recognize geometrical or numerical invariants in the diverse transformations of sensation.

I have argued in Chapter 3 that mathematics alone cannot furnish satisfactory principles of unity for material objects, but perhaps one can grant that function in the context of the phantasmagoric array of mere ideas that confronts the *cogito* of Meditation II, immersed in its first-person perspective. However, a deeper problem lies here. The *cogito* cannot have the idea of extension at this point in the order of reasons, when it has not yet established any form of alterity, including the alterity of spatial side-by-sideness. To put it another way, a consciousness that does not know itself as embedded in spatial extension cannot be acquainted with Euclidean geometry and its characteristic problems: how points bound lines and lines bound polygons, etc. Recall that in the order of reasons, the assertion of a truth at any point must depend upon and be conditioned by only what has preceded it in the order.

Descartes wants to construct a complete system of knowledge which is wholly immanent in the self-certainty contained in the clear and distinct intellect. His extraction of the concepts of substance, duration, and number from the *cogito's* reflection on itself seems at least plausible. But the geometrical ideas of extension and figure cannot be immanent in the disembodied, aspatial intellect alone. Descartes's starting-point, the *cogito*, is so impoverished that he is forced to enrich it in illicit ways. Here I argue that he has smuggled in acquaintance with a kind of alterity, externality or spatial outness. In the same way he is forced to bring in theorems about circles and triangles at the very beginning of the *Geometry*, because otherwise he would not be able to generate anything at all out of his collection of straight line segments in strict accordance with the order of reasons. Even so, his impoverished starting-points tend to impoverish his geometry, as I try to show in Chapters 2 and 5 by comparing it with the work of his contemporaries. So too, I would argue, the spiritualized epistemology that emerges from the *Meditations* is impoverished.

Even granting that the *cogito* is entitled to its purely mathematical idea of extension, one must wonder how this idea, which has a finite amount of objective reality, can in Meditation VI come to stand in relation to sensation, which has only an infinitesimal amount. Gueroult admits that for Descartes no common measure exists between them; they are disproportionate.[26] But how can mathematical invariants be instantiated in sensation and thus serve as subjectively valid conditions of the possibility of our representations of objects? Is sensation cognitively structured, or not? If it is, why does Descartes assign it such a low degree of objective reality, radically disproportionate to that of the mathematicals? If it is not, how could it ever exhibit mathematical invariants? Indeed, if the infinitesimal amount of objective reality in sensation signals to the self (albeit with merely subjective force) that something lies beyond it which is essentially distinct from it, how is that *sensum* knowable?[27]

Considerations like this lead Jean Laporte (to whom *Descartes selon l'ordre des raisons* is dedicated) to argue that the knowledge of extension must stem from the idea of the substantial union of the body and the soul introduced in Meditation VI.[28] For only on this supposition does the self's understanding of extension make sense, given the 'repugnance' of the essence of extension to the essence of spirit. Otherwise, Laporte contends, Descartes runs up against an impenetrable mystery about representation. Grant that the idea of extension is not itself extended; then how can it represent extension?

How can there be a purely spiritual representation of what fundamentally excludes mind? More generally, how is it possible for ideas to have a representative function in the first place?[29] Gueroult has two kinds of responses to this very difficult dilemma posed by Laporte. And he must have a response, since Laporte's interpretation sees Descartes as violating the order of reasons, and indeed Gueroult's reconstruction of the argument of the *Meditations* depends on the knowability of extension by spirit alone. Neither response, however, do I find convincing. The first is that Laporte's questions raise issues that Descartes is simply not obligated to address.

No doubt, one could ask oneself how it is that the mind perceives the picture as a copy and how a purely spiritual picture of what radically excludes the mind is possible. But these are questions that Descartes has not seen fit to ask or to resolve, because, according to him, they exceed the limits of our capabilities. This property of the idea to represent formal reality by its objective reality as a picture is the constitutive character that allows us to distinguish it immediately from other thoughts. It is a first given that is revealed to us by natural light, before which every investigation stops . . .

The problem for Descartes has never been to explain how the idea is originally posited as the representation of an object, but to examine in what way I can have a clear and distinct representation of this object (the problem of method), and how I can prove that such an idea has an objective validity (the problem of the critique of knowledge and metaphysics.)[30]

While it may be true that Cartesian method structures the whole enterprise of the *Meditations*, I do not see that its presuppositions are thereby no longer open to question. That the starting-points of an investigation are grounded only in intuition, that they need no accompanying logos that might embed them in a tradition or inferential context, is one of the presuppositions that I have tried to criticize all through this book. Gueroult does not defend it here, but only restates it.

Gueroult's second response is to show that Descartes in fact provides a referent for the idea of extension in Meditation V that is not *res extensa*, material extension, but something else in the category of spirit. Then of course the question of how the idea is proportional to its object is answered. Meditation V establishes the objective validity of the mathematicals as essences before their objective validity relative to existing material things is settled in

Meditation VI. The thinking self discovers in Meditation III that the internal characteristics of the idea of God reveal not only His existence (as cause of the idea) but His essence (as maximal perfection). Likewise, once the spectre of hyperbolic doubt has been banished, the intrinsic properties of the mathematicals entail their existence whether or not anything exists corresponding to them in the material realm.

The internal characteristics of the idea of God, necessarily entailing his existence, testify at the same time to the character of essence of that idea and later to the character of essence of mathematical ideas. The discovery in these ideas of a sufficient quantity of objective reality accounts for the natural certainty of the understanding in this respect. The rule of attribution of objective validity therefore remains finally in conformity with the requirements of mathematism, since it is founded entirely on the internal rationality of the notion. And it happens that the only ideas having true objective validity, meaning being the faithful pictures of an archetype, are precisely mathematical ideas or, more generally, the clear and distinct ideas that are not defined by themselves as reflections of objects existing in nature.[31]

The mathematicals reveal rational realities, essences, with an existence independent of nature.

If these essences cannot yet be located in the disembodied mind of the thinker or in nature, I infer that they must be located as ideas in the mind of God. Gueroult never comes to this conclusion explicitly, and Laporte denies the possibility referring to a letter written perhaps to Mersenne (27 May 1630),[32] where Descartes explains that though eternal truths are to be understood as essences whose author is God, they are not His emanations. It is hard to see, however, what other location they could have. But then Descartes comes perilously close to the Malebranchean position of 'seeing all things in God'; indeed he shares with Malebranche, Berkeley, and the late Leibnitz the same metaphysical risk, that with the elimination of matter the creation collapses back into the Creator. For what the disembodied self knows, in its acquaintance with the mathematicals, would be the contents of another mind; the divine mind and the human mind are fused. This seems to me epistemologically unsound, and furthermore incompatible with the integrity of the human self. The self without spatial externality and materiality dissolves in God like a tear in the ocean.

In any case, Descartes does not linger on this line of argumentation, perhaps because he senses the dangerous metaphysical impoverishment his starting-point of the *cogito* is about to inflict on his system, assimilating everything to the category of spirit. He hastens to reintroduce sensation as the testimony of material externality in the mental world of the self in Meditation VI. Then, once God has been demonstrated to be existent and perfect, the thinker can trust the infinite activity and intelligibility of God to lift the infinitesimal objective reality of sensation to the finite realm of the knowable. On this basis, the 'substantial union' of the body and soul is introduced, which though never wholly intelligible must be accepted as a fact of our biological life, as well as the existence of *res extensa*.[33]

Thus the question of how sensation can exhibit mathematical invariants is explained because it is caused by physical objects. And our mathematical ideas, as the conditions for the possibility of our knowledge of nature, are granted a material referent. For *res extensa* really does have mathematical structure. But then the problems I raised with respect to the *Principles* in Chapter 3 reassert themselves. Where does *res extensa* get its cognitive structure, the structure of Euclidean geometry? Does God confer it, or does *res extensa* have it intrinsically? If *res extensa* has mathematical structure intrinsically, why is it disproportionate to spirit, as the archetype of Euclidean geometry in the mind of God apparently is not? If it has not, how can it be susceptible to God's structuring? The vexed relation of the *cogito* to sensation in Meditation II resurfaces here as the relation of God to His creation, material nature. The monistic thrust of Cartesian method, which tries to organize all of human knowledge as a monolithic order of reasons, sits uneasily with Descartes's radical dualism.

In sum, I do not believe that Descartes can consistently frame a convincing account of knowledge that unfolds from the *cogito*, deferring for so long the introduction of spatial externality, the body, and material nature. No more could he consistently spin out a geometry from line segments, or a physics from bits of matter in rectilinear motion. On the one hand he brings externality in surreptitiously when he needs to, and on the other hand he has bequeathed to Western philosophy an impoverished paradigm for epistemology, the isolated knower abstracted from the body, nature, and social traditions. Even though he alone is not to blame for the influence of this paradigm, he obscures its origin in the Christian doctrine of the soul on the one hand and the mechanism of early modern science on the other, by never mentioning the traditions he synthesizes in his order of reasons. He claims that all his philosophy springs from the *cogito*; and so he has got the lion's share of the blame.

POSTSCRIPT

I will end this chapter, and the book, by noting that Gueroult would dismiss many of my objections to the *Meditations* as illegitimate, since in general I advance them in the name of the body, spatiality, and materiality, against the self-sufficiency of the intellectualized *cogito* posited in Meditation II. Gueroult is convinced that Descartes's inference from *veritas rationum* to *veritas rei*, taken on its own terms, is valid. His dismissal of objections such as mine is based on an appeal to mathematics, which he supposes to instantiate the order of reasons.

For the body does not figure among the links that need to be posited in knowledge before the soul is posited. It is impossible to contest the intertwined terms in a mathematical proof by reference to a term foreign to it, nor is it possible to suppose that in a series of reasons, each of which entails the succeeding one, the last, although depending on the others, could be used to challenge the positing of those preceding it.
 . . . Thus philosophy is developed as a pure geometry, which owes all its certainty to the internal linkage of its reasons, without any reference to external reality. To invoke experience 'according to common usage' against this or that reason in the chain is as pointless as to attempt to refute the demonstrated truths of geometry in the name of experience.[34]

In Chapters 1 and 2 of this book, I have shown that indeed it is possible to contest the first stages in the order of reasons in the *Geometry* by reference to terms foreign to it. For, as I argue, terms foreign to Descartes's straight line segments, like curves, areas and volumes, numbers and infinitesimals, belong to the mathematical tradition his work is embedded in and yet are excluded by his choice of starting-points. He achieves his results only by raiding the tradition for its foreign terms when he needs them, and fails to see important consequences of his results because of his conceptual narrowings. Descartes's initial, unremarked exclusions in the *Geometry* have serious consequences for mathematics.

I also argue that developments further along in the order of reasons in fact rebound upon earlier pronouncements, and force

The Meditations Re-examined

their revision. Descartes's hasty generalizations about the hierarchy of curves and the constructibility of problems by certain curves are cases in point. And his combination of geometry, algebra, and number forces a revision both in the conceptualization of his simples, line segments, and of his own classification of curves in the work of his successors.

Not only does Descartes's *Geometry* not conform to the ideal of his method, it exhibits the mixed consequences that ideal has when it is applied to a subject-matter. If mathematics is embedded in tradition, if its amplifications are corrigible, if its simples are not so simple, its complexes in need of an account of their integrity, and its abstract relational structures not so transparent, all the more so will philosophy prove to be a creature of tradition whose syntheses are not only creative but revisable. Cartesian method is reductive, and reduction has proved to be a powerful instrument in mathematics and physics. But the philosopher is well advised to exercise caution when turning that same instrument upon the complexities of nature and human social life.

Notes

1. Three especially well-done examples of this approach are A. Kenny, *Descartes: A Study of his Philosophy* (Studies in Philosophy; New York: Random House, 1968); Frankfurt, *Demons, Dreamers and Madmen*; and E. Curley, *Descartes Against the Skeptics* (Cambridge, Mass.: Harvard University Press, 1978).
2. See Belaval, *Leibniz critique de Descartes*, ch. 3, esp. pp. 159–72; and Grene, *Descartes*, pp. 5–7 and ch. 3. Frankfurt does acknowledge the importance of intuition for Descartes's epistemology in *Demons, Dreamers and Madmen*, pp. 152–5.
3. Vuillemin, *Nécessité ou contingence*, pp. 216–17.
4. Vuillemin, *What are Philosophical Systems?*, pp. 125–6.
5. In *Demons, Dreamers and Madmen*, ch. 11, Frankfurt contests the claim that Descartes regards thinking as the essence of a human being. But this reading is hard to reconcile with Descartes's claim at the beginning of Meditation VI, discussed below, that none of the faculties besides intellect is essential to his mind, and that he would retain his identity without them.
6. Gueroult, *Descartes selon l'ordre des raisons*, i. 127–38; Ariew, *Descartes' Philosophy*, i. 80–9. The *Meditations* was first published in Latin, in Paris, 1641. It was published the next year in Amsterdam with the complete 'Objections and Replies' appended; this is the version reprinted in Adam and Tannery, vol. vii. It was translated into French in 1642 by the Duc de Luynes. For each citation, I will give the volume and page numbers of the English translation in Haldane and Ross, and then the page number from vol. vii of Adam and Tannery.
7. This is essentially Vuillemin's argument in sect. 16 of *Mathématiques et métaphysique chez Descartes*.
8. Gueroult, *Descartes selon l'ordre des raisons*, ii. 7–21; Ariew, *Descartes' Philosophy*, ii. 3–15.
9. Gueroult, *Descartes selon l'ordre des raisons*, i. 194–203; Ariew, *Descartes' Philosophy*, i. 133–40. It is worth mentioning that Curley in *Descartes Against the Skeptics*, ch. 6, and B. Williams in *Descartes: The Project of Pure Enquiry* (Atlantic Highlands, N.J.: Humanities Press, 1978), ch. 5, find Descartes's proofs of the existence of God inadequate. Curley disputes Gueroult's position in detail. My general sense is that their attacks seem stronger than they are because of their tendency to treat Meditations III and V as collections of propositions rather than the experience of a self constructing a domain of knowledge. My own difficulty with Descartes's proofs is that the self's confrontation with God is given in wholly universal terms; I do not think the self's

particularity can be left out of such an account. But that is a topic for another essay.
10. Gueroult, *Descartes selon l'ordre des raisons*, i. 213–16 and 331–4; Ariew, *Descartes' Philosophy*, i. 148–50 and 237–40.
11. Gueroult, *Descartes selon l'ordre des raisons*, i. 216–21; Ariew, *Descartes' Philosophy*, i. 150–4.
12. *Meditationes*, i. 153; 28.
13. B. L. Mijuskovic explores these presuppositions and how they figure in Descartes's philosophy in 'The Achilles of Rationalist Arguments', *Archives Internationales d'Histoire des Idées*, 13 (1974), esp. 22–33.
14. *Meditationes*, i. 154–7; 30–4.
15. Ibid. i. 151–2; 26–7.
16. See *inter alia* the letters to Mersenne, 1 Apr. 1640 and 6 Aug. 1640, AM iv. 45–9 and 130–4. Wilson has a useful discussion of the status of the imagination in Meditation v in *Descartes*, pp. 168–72.
17. *Meditationes*, i. 153; 28.
18. *Objectiones Quintae*, ii. 139–40; 261–3.
19. Ibid. ii. 144; 268.
20. *Quintae Responsiones*, ii. 211–12; 358–9.
21. Gueroult, *Descartes selon l'ordre des raisons* i. 66–7; Ariew, *Descartes' Philosophy*, i. 37–8.
22. Wilson in *Descartes*, pp. 198–200, also points out that Descartes has difficulty explaining how one knows oneself as a particular.
23. *Meditationes*, i. 165; 44–5.
24. AM iv. 222–5.
25. Gueroult, *Descartes selon l'ordre des raisons* i. 133; Ariew, *Descartes' Philosophy*, i. 85. See also the larger discussion in Gueroult, i. 132–8; Ariew, i. 84–9.
26. Gueroult, *Descartes selon l'ordre des raisons* i. 140–1; Ariew, *Descartes' Philosophy*, i. 90–1.
27. Wilson in *Descartes*, pp. 202–4, makes a related point about the paucity of cognitive significance in sensation according to Descartes.
28. J. Laporte, *Le Rationalisme de Descartes* (Paris: Presses Universitaires de France, 1950), ch. 4.
29. Ibid. 128.
30. Gueroult, *Descartes selon l'ordre des raisons*, i. 141; Ariew, *Descartes' Philosophy*, i. 91.
31. Gueroult, *Descartes selon l'ordre des raisons*, i. 216; Ariew, *Descartes' Philosophy*, i. 150.
32. AM i. 141–3; Laporte, *Rationalisme de Descartes*, pp. 118–19.
33. Gueroult, *Descartes selon l'ordre des raisons*, ii. 14–18; Ariew, *Descartes' Philosophy*, ii. 8–12.
34. Gueroult, *Descartes selon l'ordre des raisons*, i. 20–1; Ariew, *Descartes' Philosophy*, i. 6–7.

Bibliography

Primary Sources

DESCARTES, R., *Correspondance*, ed. C. Adam and G. Milhaud (8 vols.; Paris: Félix Alcan, 1936).
—— *The Geometry of René Descartes*, ed. D. E. Smith and M. L. Latham (New York: Dover, 1954).
—— *Œuvres*, ed. C. Adam and P. Tannery (12 vols.; new ed., Paris: Vrin, 1964–74).
—— *The Philosophical Works of Descartes*, ed. E. S. Haldane and G. R. T. Ross (2 vols.; Cambridge: Cambridge University Press, 1967).
—— *Treatise of Man*, ed. T. S. Hall (Cambridge, Mass.: Harvard University Press, 1972).
—— *Principles of Philosophy*, ed. V. R. Miller and R. P. Miller (Dordrecht: D. Reidel, 1983/4).

ARISTOTLE, *Physics*, ed. R. Hope (Lincoln: University of Nebraska Press, 1961).
EUCLID, *The Thirteen Books of Euclid's Elements*, ed. Sir Thomas Heath (3 vols.; New York: Dover, 1956).
FERMAT, P., *Œuvres*, ed. P. Tannery and C. Henry (4 vols.; Paris: Gauthier-Villars, 1891–1912).
GALILEI, G., *Le Opere di Galileo Galilei*, ed. A. Favaro (20 vols.; Florence: Edizione Nazionale, 1929–39).
—— *Dialogues Concerning Two New Sciences*, ed. H. Crew and A. de Salvo (New York: Dover, 1954).
LEIBNIZ, G. W., *Philosophical Papers and Letters*, ed. L. Loemker (Dordrecht: D. Reidel, 1956).
MERSENNE, M., *Correspondance*, ed. M. Tannery (16 vols.; Paris: Presses Universitaires de France, 1933–86).
NEWTON, I., *Principia*, ed. A. Motte and F. Cajori (2 vols.; Berkeley: University of California Press, 1934).

Secondary Sources

ARIEW, R., (ed.), *Descartes' Philosophy Interpreted According to the Order of Reasons* (2 vols.; Minneapolis: University of Minnesota Press, 1984).
—— 'The Infinite in Descartes' Conversation with Burman', *Archiv für Geschichte der Philosophie*, 69 (1987), 140–63.
BECK, L. J., *The Method of Descartes* (Oxford: Oxford University Press, 1952).

Bibliography

BELAVAL, Y., *Leibniz critique de Descartes* (Paris: Gallimard, 1960).

BONEVAC, D., *Reduction in the Abstract Sciences* (Cambridge, Mass.: Hackett Publishing Co., 1982).

BOS, H. J. M., 'On the Representation of Curves in Descartes' *Géométrie*', *Archive for History of the Exact Sciences*, 24 (1981), 295–338.

—— 'The Structure of Descartes' *Géométrie*', *Atti del Covegno Internazionale 'Descartes: il Discorso sul Metodo e i Saggi di questo Metodo'*, Lecce, 22–4 Oct. 1987.

BOYER, C. B., *History of Analytic Geometry* (New York: Scripta Mathematica, 1956).

—— *A History of Mathematics* (Princeton: Princeton University Press, 1985).

CHIHARA, C., *Ontology and the Vicious Circle Principle* (Ithaca: Cornell University Press, 1973).

CHURCHLAND, P., *Matter and Consciousness* (Cambridge, Mass.: MIT Press, 1988).

CLARKE, D., *Descartes' Philosophy of Science* (University Park: Pennsylvania State University Press, 1982).

CURLEY, E., *Descartes Against the Skeptics* (Cambridge, Mass.: Harvard University Press, 1978).

DE GANDT, F., 'Les *Méchaniques* attribuées à Aristote et le renouveau de la science des machines au 16e siècle', Actes du colloque, 'L'Aristotélisme au 16e siècle' in *Les Études Philosophiques*, 33 (1986), 391–405.

—— *Force et Géométrie: La théorie Newtonienne de la force centripète, présentée dans son contexte* (Doctorat d'État; Paris, 1987).

—— 'L'Analyse de la percussion chez Galilée et Torricelli' in F. De Gandt (ed.), *L'Œuvre de Torricelli* (Nice: Publications de la Faculté de Nice et Sciences Humaines de Nice, 1989), 53–77.

DRAKE, S., and DRABKIN, I. E. (eds.) *Mechanics in Sixteenth Century Italy* (Madison: University of Wisconsin Press, 1969).

FRANKFURT, H., *Demons, Dreamers and Madmen: The Defense of Reason in Descartes's Meditations* (History of Philosophy Series; Indianapolis and New York: Bobbs-Merrill, 1970).

GABBEY, A., 'Force and Inertia in the Seventeenth Century: Descartes and Newton' in S. Gaukroger (ed.), *Descartes: Philosophy, Mathematics and Physics* (Brighton: Harvester Press, 1980), 230–320.

—— 'Descartes' Physics and Descartes' Mechanics: Chicken and Egg?', forthcoming.

GARBER, D., 'Mind, Body and the Laws of Nature', *Midwest Studies in Philosophy*, 8 (1983), 105–33.

—— 'Descartes et la Méthode en 1637' in N. Grimaldi and J.-L. Marion (eds.), *Le Discours et sa Méthode* (Paris: Presses Universitaires de France, 1987), 65–87.

Bibliography

—— and COHEN, L., 'A Point of Order: Analysis, Synthesis and Descartes's *Principles*', *Archiv für Geschichte der Philosophie*, 64 (1982), 136–47.
GAUKROGER, S. (ed.), *Descartes: Philosophy, Mathematics and Physics* (Brighton: Harvester Press, 1980).
GIBSON J. J., *The Ecological Approach to Visual Perception* (Boston: Houghton Mifflin Co., 1979).
GOLDMAN, A., *Epistemology and Cognition* (Cambridge, Mass.: Harvard University Press, 1986).
GRENE, M., *Descartes* (Philosophers in Context; Minneapolis: University of Minnesota Press, 1985).
GROSHOLZ, E., 'Wittgenstein and the Correlation of Logic and Arithmetic', *Ratio*, 23 (1981), 31–42.
—— 'Leibniz's Unification of Geometry with Algebra and Dynamics', *Studia Leibnitiana*, Special Issue 13 (1984), 198–208.
—— 'Two Episodes in the Unification of Logic and Topology', *British Journal for the Philosophy of Science*, 36 (1985), 147–57.
—— 'Some Uses of Proportion in Newton's *Principia*, Book I: A Case Study in Applied Mathematics', *Studies in the History and Philosophy of Science*, (1987), 209–20.
GUEROULT, M., *Descartes selon l'ordre des raisons* (2 vols.; Paris: Aubier, Éditions Montaigne, 1968).
HACKING, I., 'Proof and Eternal Truths: Descartes and Leibniz' in S. Gaukroger (ed.), *Descartes: Philosophy, Mathematics and Physics* (Brighton: Harvester Press, 1980), 169–80.
HATFIELD, G., 'First Philosophy and Natural Philosophy in Descartes' in A. J. Holland (ed.), *Philosophy, Its History and Historiography* (Dordrecht: D. Reidel, 1985), 149–64.
—— 'Science, Certainty and Descartes', *PSA 1988*, 2 (East Lansing: Philosophy of Science Association, 1989).
HOFFMAN, J., 'Über Auftauschen und Behandlung von Differentialgleichungen im 17. Jahrhundert', *Humanismus und Technik*, 15 (1972), 1–40.
KENNY, A., *Descartes: A Study of his Philosophy* (Studies in Philosophy; New York: Random House, 1968).
KIMBROUGH, S. O., 'On the Reduction of Genetics to Molecular Biology', *Philosophy of Science*, 46 (1979), 389–406.
KOYRÉ, A., *La loi de la chute des corps: Descartes et Galilée, Études Galiléennes*, ii (Paris: Hermann, 1939).
LAPORTE, J., *Le Rationalisme de Descartes* (Paris: Presses Universitaires de France, 1950).
MAHONEY, M., 'The Beginnings of Algebraic Thought in the Seventeenth Century' in S. Gaukroger (ed.), *Descartes: Philosophy, Mathematics and Physics* (Brighton: Harvester Press, 1980), 141–55.
MARION, J.-L., *Sur l'ontologie grise de Descartes* (Paris: Vrin, 1975).

MAULL, N., 'Unifying Science without Reduction', *Studies in History and Philosophy of Science*, 8 (1977), 143–62.
—— and DARDEN, L., 'Interfield Theories', *Philosophy of Science*, 44 (1977), 43–64.
MIJUSKOVIC, B. L., 'The Achilles of Rationalist Arguments', *Archives Internationales d'Histoire des Idées*, 13 (1974).
MILLIKAN, R. G., *Language, Thought and Other Biological Categories* (Cambridge, Mass.: MIT Press, 1984).
MOLLAND, A. G., 'Shifting the Foundations: Descartes' Transformation of Ancient Geometry', *Historia Mathematica*, 3 (1976), 21–49.
—— 'The Atomisation of Motion: A Facet of the Scientific Revolution', *Studies in History and Philosophy of Science*, 13 (1982), 31–54.
NAGEL, E., *The Structure of Science* (New York: Harcourt, Brace & World, 1961).
NICKLES, T., 'Theory Generalization, Problem Reduction and the Unity of Science' in R. S. Cohen *et al.* (eds.), *PSA 1974* (Dordrecht: D. Reidel, 1976), 33–75.
QUINE, W. V. O., *From a Logical Point of View* (New York: Harper & Row, 1963).
SCHOULS, P., *The Imposition of Method: A Study of Descartes and Locke* (Oxford: Clarendon Press, 1980).
SCRIBA, C., 'Zur Lösung des 2. Debeauneschen Problems durch Descartes', *Archive for History of Exact Sciences*, 1 (1960–2), 406–19.
SHAPERE, D., 'Scientific Theories and their Domains' in F. Suppe (ed.), *The Structure of Scientific Theories* (Urbana: University of Illinois Press, 1974), 518–65.
SKLAR, L., 'Types of Inter-Theoretic Reduction', *British Journal for Philosophy of Science*, 18 (1967), 109–24.
SMIGELSKIS, D., 'Namings, Showings and the Analytic Achievements of Appreciation', unpublished paper.
SYLLA, E., 'Compounding Ratios' in E. Mendelsohn (ed.), *Transformation and Tradition in the Sciences* (Cambridge: Cambridge University Press, 1984), 11–43.
—— 'Galileo and the Oxford Calculators', *Studies in Philosophy and the History of Philosophy*, 15, 53–108.
VUILLEMIN, J., *Mathématiques et métaphysique chez Descartes* (Paris: Presses Universitaires de France, 1960).
—— *Nécessité ou contingence: L'aporie de Diodore et les systèmes philosophiques* (Paris: Éditions de Minuit, 1984).
—— *What are Philosophical Systems?* (Cambridge: Cambridge University Press, 1986).
WESTFALL, R., *The Construction of Modern Science* (New York: John Wiley & Sons, 1971).

WILLIAMS, B., *Descartes: The Project of Pure Enquiry* (Atlantic Highlands, NJ: Humanities Press, 1978).

WILSON, M., *Descartes* (Arguments of the Philosophers Series; London: Routledge & Kegan Paul, 1978).

YOLTON, J., *Perceptual Acquaintance from Descartes to Reid* (Minneapolis: University of Minnesota Press, 1984).

Index

algebra 20–1, 32, 39, 56–7
animal spirits, see subtle matter
Archimedean axiom, see Eudoxian
 axiom
Ariew, R. 9, 13 n., 98 n.
Aristotle 8, 59 n., 72, 80–1
Arnauld 125, 130, 132 n.
Augustine 142

Bacon, R. 53
Beck, L. J. 5
Beeckman 103
Belaval, Y. 11–12 n., 59 n., 150 n.
Berkeley 146
biology, Cartesian, see Treatise of Man
Bonevac, D. 12 n.
Bos, H. J. M. 37 n., 59 n.
Boyer, C. B. 37 n.
brain:
 in Descartes' theory of perception
 122–7

Campanus 53
Cartesian circle 134
Cartesian parabola 46–50
Chihara, C. 13–14 n.
Churchland, Patricia 10
Churchland, Paul 10, 14 n.
circularity, problem of:
 in Cartesian geometry 22–5, 40–3
 in Cartesian metaphysics 134
 in Cartesian physics 69–70
Clarke, D. 14 n., 78 n., 131 n.
cogito 135–48
Cohen, L. 13 n., 78 n.
cosmogony, Cartesian 61, 63–4, 91–4
Curley, E. 150–1 n.
curves:
 as complexes for geometry 16–18,
  22, 57–8, 84, 149
 corresponding to equations in two
  unknowns 7–8, 43, 48
 hierarchy of 29, 43–50
 as hybrids 27, 50, 58, 112–14, 139
 as Pappian loci 29, 34–5, 43
 in physics 82, 107–9, 112–14
 as traced by mechanical devices 38–49

Dante 142
Darden, L. 12 n.
Da Vinci 80
Debeaune's Problem 53–5
De Gandt, F. 98 n., 110, 116 n.
Descartes, R.:
 as critical 2, 136
 as intuitionist 2, 133–6, 138, 145
 as reductionist see reduction
Discourse on Method 3, 5–7, 15–16
domains, partial unification of 3,
  12–13 n., 58, 60 n., 61–4, 66–7,
  99–101, 103, 114, 118, 127–30,
  134–5, 149
Drabkin, I. E. 98 n.
Drake, S. 98 n.

Epicurus 2
Euclid 18–19, 21, 23, 25, 50–2
Euclidean space 64–7, 97
Eudoxian axiom 50–2
extension, idea of 65, 142–7

faculties, see intellect; imagination;
 memory; sensation
Fermat 27, 28
Ferrari's rule 46
first element matter, see subtle matter
force 87–8, 105–9, 113–14
Frankfurt, H. 9, 11 n., 150 n.
free fall 101–9

Gabbey, A. 78 n., 110, 115 n.
Galen 120–2
Galileo 20, 80, 99–116
Garber, D. 11 n., 13 n., 78 n.
Gassendi 123, 140–1
Gaukroger, S. 12 n.
genre, see curves, hierarchy of
Geometry 8, 15–60, 63, 70, 76, 134,
  138–9, 144, 148–9
geometry, Cartesian 15–60, 63–77; see
 also Geometry
geometry, classical 18–19, 21, 23,
  25–7, 29–32, 50–2, 65, 113, 143
Gibson, J. J. 131 n.

Index

God:
  as a physical cause 62–4, 68–71, 87, 96
  as a biological cause 128
  as guarantor of certainty 136–7, 146
  as source of mathematical ideas 147
Goldman, A. 14
Grene, M. 9, 13 n., 150 n.
Grosholz, E. 13 n., 60 n., 115 n.
Gueroult, M. 4, 9, 13 n., 78 n., 135–7, 141, 143–9, 150–1 n.

Hacking, I. 12 n.
Hatfield, G. 14 n., 131 n.
Heron of Alexandria 80
Hoffman, J. 60 n.
homogeneity:
  of starting points 3, 55–6, 62–4, 68, 76, 81, 92, 100–1, 118, 127, 134–6, 140–2
  of terms in proportions 50–3
Huygens, C. 75, 110
hybrids 27, 50, 58, 100–1, 112–14, 139

imagination 138–42
individuation 65, 69–71, 85, 130, 138–42, 146–7
intellect 138–44

Kant 2, 4
Kenny, A. 150
Kepler:
  law of areas 113
Kimbrough, S. O. 131 n.
Koyré, A. 99–105, 111, 115–16 n.

Laporte, J. 144–6
laws of motion 69, 80–98, 123–4
Leibniz 10, 19–20, 21, 27, 55–6, 58, 75, 100, 103

Mahoney, M. 59 n.
Malebranche 146
Marion, J. L. 13
mathematics:
  and Cartesian method 3, 135–7, 146, 148–9;
  and Cartesian physics 60–79, 80–1, 99–101, 143–7
Maull, N. 12 n., 131 n.
mechanism:
  in Cartesian biology 117–32
  in Cartesian physics 107, 115 n., 117, 121
  Meditations 1, 4, 9, 61, 67, 117, 130, 133–51
  memory 138–42
  intellectual 140
Mersenne 99, 104, 105, 110, 112–13, 146
method, Cartesian 1–5, 7–9, 11 n., 15–18:
  as analytic 5–7, 13 n., 78 n.
  in biology 117–19
  in geometry 25–6, 38–40, 50, 57–8
  as intuitionist 2, 133–6, 138, 145
  in the Meditations 133–5, 148–9
  in physics 63–4, 76–7, 80–1, 95–7, 99–101, 111–2, 114
Mijuskovic, B. L. 151 n.
Millikan, R. G. 14 n.
Molland, A. G. 37 n., 115 n.
momento 80, 102–3, 110–11
momentum, conservation of 87–8, 90–1, 107
More, H. 63, 78 n.
motion 63–4, 68–70, 72–5, 101–16
  see also unity of common motion

Nagel, E. 12 n.
Nemorarius 53
Newton:
  Principia 8, 78 n., 100, 108–9, 113–14
Nickles, T. 12 n.

order of reasons 2, 6, 15, 25–6, 41–2, 61–2, 78 n., 99, 111, 135–8, 141–3, 148–9
optical ovals 49–50

Pappus's Problem 29–32
  and classification of cases (curves) 34–5
  and classification of cases (problems) 33–4;
patterns:
  in Cartesian biology 126–30
pineal gland 125–9
plenum:
  in Aristotle 81
  in Cartesian physics 64–5, 81–5, 109
principle of virtual work 110
Principles 8, 61–97, 100, 107, 109–10, 112, 117–19, 129–30, 134, 139

Index

problems:
as complexes for geometry 16, 38–40, 43–4, 46, 48–9
corresponding to equations in one unknown 28, 46, 48
hierarchy of 33–5, 38–40
projectile motion 108, 112–14
proportion:
in the *Geometry* 16, 20, 50–7
in the *Meditations* 136–7, 139–40, 144–7
in relation to method 7, 99
physics:
Cartesian see *Principles*

Quine, W. V. O. 10, 13 n.

ratios 36 n., 50–3
reduction 2–3, 12–13 n., 7–10
in Cartesian biology 117–19, 127–30
in Cartesian geometry 17–18, 27, 42–50, 55–8, 111–12
in Cartesian metaphysics 134–5, 148–9
in Cartesian physics 64, 76–7, 96, 99–101, 114
Renaissance Naturalism 123
res extensa 61–71, 81, 85–6, 94–7, 112–13, 122–3, 136, 139, 142–8
and divisibility 85, 91–6
and impenetrability 85–8, 96
Roberval 111
rules of impact 87–91, 107, 118, 127, 129–30

Schouls, P. 13 n.
Science, Cartesian 6, 72, 123
see also *Principles*; *Treatise of Man*
Scriba, C. 60 n.
second element matter 92, 112, 130

sensation 137–47
Shapere, D. 12–13 n., 79 n.
simple machines, theory of 80–1, 100, 109–12, 118, 130
Sklar, L. 12 n.
Smigelski, D. 36 n.
starting points 16
in geometry 16, 19–21, 32, 46, 100, 139, 149
in metaphysics 134–5, 145–9
in physics 61–77, 95–7, 101, 107
straight line segments 82, 107
see also starting-points in geometry
substantial union 142, 144–7
subtle matter 84–5, 90–3, 96, 118–19, 123–9
Sylla, E. 36 n., 60 n.

Tannery, P. 99
Theon 53
third element matter 93–4, 118–20, 130
Torricelli 80, 100, 111
tracing-machines, Cartesian 38–49
Treatise of Man 9, 117–32, 134

unity in Cartesian physics
of common motion 68–71, 73–6, 80, 86–7, 94–5, 130, 139
of shape 66–7, 71, 73, 91, 94–5
vortex theory 81–4, 112, 118

Vuillemin, J. 4–5, 7, 11 n., 60 n., 99, 115 n., 150 n.

Westfall, R. 131 n.
Williams, B. 150–1 n.
Wilson, M. 9, 11 n., 151 n.

Yolton, J. 132 n.